ROOKIE COACHES SKI RACING GUIDE

American Coaching Effectiveness Program

in cooperation with the
U.S. Ski Coaches Association

Human Kinetics Publishers

Library of Congress Cataloging-in-Publication Data

American Coaching Effectiveness Program.
   Rookie coaches ski racing guide / American Coaching Effectiveness
Program in association with the U.S. Ski Coaches Association.
      p.   cm.
   ISBN 0-87322-550-3
   1. Skiing for children--Coaching.   2. Ski racing--Coaching.
I. United States Ski Coaches Association.   II. Title.
GV854.32.A44   1994
796.93--dc20   93-11877
                                                        CIP

ISBN 0-87322-550-3

Developmental Editor: Kelly Hill
Managing Editor: Jan Colarusso Seeley
Ski Racing Consultant: Deb LaMarche, U.S. Ski Coaches Association
Assistant Editors: Julie Lancaster, Dawn Roselund, and Lisa Sotirelis
Copyeditor: Laurie McGee
Proofreaders: Julia Anderson and Dawn Barker
Production Director: Ernie Noa
Typesetter: Ruby Zimmerman
Text Designer: Keith Blomberg
Layout Artist: Tara Welsch
Cover Design: Jack Davis
Cover Photo: Lori Adamski-Peek
Interior Art: Tim Stiles, cartoons; Tom Janowski, Mac art; Sharon Barner, line drawings; and Debra Dietz, art
   consultant
Printer: United Graphics

Human Kinetics books are available at special discounts for bulk purchase. Special editions or book excerpts can also be created to specification. For details, contact the Special Sales Manager at Human Kinetics.

Printed in the United States of America   10 9 8 7 6 5 4 3 2 1

Human Kinetics Publishers
Box 5076, Champaign, IL 61825-5076
1-800-747-4457

Canada: Human Kinetics Publishers, Box 24040, Windsor, ON N8Y 4Y9
1-800-465-7301 (in Canada only)

Europe: Human Kinetics Publishers (Europe) Ltd., P.O. Box IW14, Leeds LS16 6TR, England
0532-781708

Australia: Human Kinetics Publishers, P.O. Box 80, Kingswood 5062, South Australia
618-374-0433

New Zealand: Human Kinetics Publishers, P.O. Box 105-231, Auckland 1
(09) 309-2259

Contents

A Message From the United States Ski Coaches Association

As the Director of Coaches Education for the United States Ski Coaches Association (USSCA), I applaud your interest in helping young Americans enjoy the fun and challenge of ski racing. As a ski racing coach, you'll be introducing a sport to children that they can enjoy for the rest of their lives. Today people compete in ski racing into their sixties and seventies.

The *Rookie Coaches Ski Racing Guide* will be a valuable resource to get you started in ski coaching. USSCA has also designed a Rookie Coaches Clinic Program to further assist the new coach. The guide and clinic together will address your concerns as a novice coach.

The Rookie Coaches clinics are the first introduction to an ongoing program of education, training, and experience for ski coaches at all levels of skiing in the United States. I encourage you to become a member of USSCA and get involved with the formal training programs it has to offer. USSCA can assist you in growing and developing your skills as a ski coach. You have a tremendous impact on the lives of young skiers and their long-term interest in ski racing.

On behalf of the United States Ski Coaches Association, I welcome you to coaching and hope you find your new role rewarding.

Tim Ross
Director of Coaches Education

Welcome to Coaching!

Coaching young ski racers is an exciting way to be involved in skiing. But it isn't always easy. Some coaches are overwhelmed by the responsibilities of helping athletes through their early sport experiences. And it's not surprising, because coaching young athletes requires a lot more than just watching your skiers fly down the slopes! It involves preparing them physically and mentally to compete effectively, fairly, and safely in their sport, and providing them with a positive role model.

The *Rookie Coaches Ski Racing Guide* will help you meet the challenges and experience the many rewards of coaching young athletes. We prepared this practical resource for adults with little or no formal training in coaching ski racing. In this guide, you'll learn how to apply coaching principles and teach fundamental skiing and racing skills to young athletes.

The American Coaching Effectiveness Program (ACEP) would like to thank Deb LaMarche and the United States Ski Coaches Association (USSCA) for contributing considerable ski racing expertise to this guide. This book also serves as a text for ACEP's Rookie Coaches Course and is part of the USSCA Coaches Education Program.

Again, welcome to coaching. If we can help you meet the challenges of your role with information, materials, or courses, please contact us.

ACEP
Box 5076
Champaign, IL 61825-5076
1-800-747-5698

United States Ski Coaches Association
P.O. Box 100
Park City, UT 84060
1-801-649-9090

Good coaching!

UNIT 1

Who, Me . . . a Coach?

If you're like most youth ski team coaches, you were probably recruited from the ranks of concerned parents, skiing enthusiasts, or former racers. And, like many rookie and veteran coaches, you probably have had little formal instruction on how to coach. But when the call went out for coaches to assist with the local ski racing program, you answered because you like children, enjoy ski racing, are community-minded, or perhaps are interested in starting a coaching career.

I Want to Help, But . . .

Your initial coaching assignment may be difficult. Like many new alpine ski coaches, you may not know everything there is to know about ski racing, or about how to work with children. Relax; this *Rookie Coaches Ski Racing Guide* will help you learn the basics of coaching ski racing effectively. In the coming pages you will find the answers to such common questions as these:

• What tools do I need to be a good coach?

- How can I best communicate with my skiers?
- How do I go about teaching skiing skills?
- What can I do to promote safety?
- What actions do I take when someone is injured?
- What are the basic rules for ski racing?
- How do I teach the skills and strategies of ski racing?
- What practice drills will improve my skiers' skills?

Before answering these questions, let's take a look at what's involved in being a coach.

Am I a Parent or a Coach?

Many coaches are parents, but the two roles should not be confused. As a parent you are responsible only to yourself and your child; as a coach you are responsible to the organization and to all the skiers on the team (including your child) and their parents. Because of these additional responsibilities, your behavior on the ski hill will be different than it is at home, and your son or daughter may not understand why. Take these steps to avoid problems when coaching your child:

- Ask your child if she or he wants you to coach the team.
- Explain why you wish to be involved with the team.

- Discuss with your child your new responsibilities and how they will affect your relationship when coaching.
- Limit your "coach" behavior to those times when you are in a coaching role.
- Avoid parenting during practice or race situations to keep your role clear in your child's mind.
- Reaffirm your love for your child irrespective of his or her performance on the ski slopes.

What Are My Responsibilities as a Coach?

A coach assumes the responsibility of doing everything possible to ensure that the youngsters on his or her team will have an enjoyable and safe experience while they learn ski racing skills. If you're ever in doubt about your approach, remind yourself that "fun and fundamentals" are most important.

Provide an Enjoyable Experience

Alpine ski racing should be fun. Even if nothing else is accomplished, make certain your skiers have fun. Take the fun out of ski racing and you'll take the kids out of the sport. Children enter sport for a number of reasons (e.g., to meet and ski with other children, to develop physically, to learn skills), but their major objective is to have fun. Help them satisfy this goal by injecting humor and variety into your practices. Also, make competitions nonthreatening, festive experiences for your skiers. Such an approach will increase their desire to participate in the future. Kids who have fun continue to participate much longer than kids who don't share in this positive experience. Unit 2 will help you learn how to satisfy your skiers' yearning for fun and keep winning in perspective. And Unit 3 will describe how to communicate this perspective effectively to them.

Provide a Safe Experience

You are responsible for planning and teaching activities in such a way that the progression between activities minimizes risks (see Units 4 and 5). Further, you must ensure

that the ski slopes on which your team practices and competes are reasonably protected from hazards, and that your skiers' equipment meets current safety standards. Finally, you need to protect yourself from any legal liability issues that might arise from your involvement as a coach. Unit 5 will help you take the appropriate precautions.

Teach Basic Ski Racing Skills

In becoming a coach, you take on the role of educator. You must teach your skiers the fundamental skills and strategies necessary for success in ski racing. That means you need to "go to school." If you don't know the basics of ski racing now, you can learn them by reading Units 6, 7, and 8 of this manual. Even if you know ski racing as a competitor, do you know how to teach it? This book will help you get started. You'll also find it easier to provide good educational experiences for your skiers if you plan your practices. Unit 4 of this manual provides guidelines for effective practice planning, and Units 7 and 8 will give you help designing your practice sessions.

Who Can Help?

Veteran coaches in your ski area are an especially good source of information and

assistance. So are professional ski instructors. These coaches have experienced the same emotions and concerns you are facing; their advice and feedback can be invaluable as you work through your first few years of coaching. You can also learn a great deal by observing local ski coaches at practices and competitions. You might even ask a few of the coaches you respect most to lend a hand with a couple of your practices.

You can get additional help by attending ski racing clinics, reading ski racing publications, and studying instructional videos. Contact ACEP, or write or call the

United States Ski Coaches Association
P.O. Box 100
Park City, UT 84060
801-649-9090

Coaching ski racing is a rewarding experience. And, just as you want your skiers to learn and practice to be the best they can be, learn all you can about coaching to become the best ski coach you can be.

UNIT 2

What Tools Do I Need to Coach?

o you have the traditional ski coaching tools—skis, a warm parka, a stopwatch, and a power drill? They'll help you coach, but to be a successful coach you'll need five other tools that cannot be bought. These tools are available only through self-examination and hard work, but they're easy to remember with the acronym COACH:

C—Comprehension
O—Outlook
A—Affection
C—Character
H—Humor

Comprehension

Comprehension of the rules, skills, and tactics of ski racing is required. To assist you in learning about ski racing, the second half of this guide describes rules, skills, and tactics and suggests how to plan for the season and individual practices. You'll also find a variety of drills and progressions to use in developing young athletes' skiing and racing skills.

To improve your comprehension of ski racing, take the following steps:

- Read Units 6, 7, and 8 of this book.
- Consider studying other ski coaching books and videos.
- Contact the United States Ski Coaches Association at (801) 649-9090.
- Attend ski coaches' clinics.
- Talk with other, more experienced ski coaches.
- Observe local United States Ski Association–sanctioned events.
- Watch ski races on television.

In addition to having ski racing knowledge, you must implement proper training and safety methods so your skiers can participate with little risk of injury. Even then, sport injuries will occur. More often than not, you'll be the first person responding to your athletes' injuries. Therefore, make sure you understand the basic emergency care procedures described in Unit 5. Also read in that unit how to handle more serious sport injury situations.

Outlook

Outlook refers to your perspective and goals—what you are seeking as a coach. The most common coaching objectives are (a) to have fun, (b) to help ski racers develop their physical, mental, and social skills, and (c) to win. Thus, outlook involves the priorities you set, your planning, and your vision for the future.

To work successfully with children in a sport setting, you must have your priorities in order. How do you rank the importance of fun, development, and winning? Check yourself. Answer the following questions to examine your objectives.

Which situation would make you most proud?

a. Knowing that each participant enjoyed ski racing

b. Seeing that all skiers improved their ski racing skills
c. Winning the division championship

Which statement best reflects your thoughts about sport?

a. If it isn't fun, don't do it.
b. Everyone should learn something every day.
c. Ski racing isn't fun if you don't win.

How would you like your ski racers to remember you?

a. As a coach who was fun to ski with
b. As a coach who provided a good base of fundamental skills
c. As a coach who had a winning record

Which would you most like to hear a parent of a child on your team say?

a. Michael really had a good time ski racing this year.
b. Nina learned some important lessons ski racing this year.
c. Jake raced on the first-place ski team this year.

Which of the following would be the most rewarding moment of your season?

a. Having your team not want to stop skiing even after practice is over
b. Observing your skiers finally master the skill of skiing comfortably through tough terrain
c. Winning the division championship

Look over your answers. If you most often selected "a" responses, then having fun is most important to you. A majority of "b" answers suggests that skill development is what attracts you to coaching. And if "c" was your most frequent response, winning is tops on your list of coaching priorities.

Most coaches say fun and development are more important, but when actually coaching, some coaches emphasize—indeed over-emphasize—winning. You too will face situations that challenge you to keep winning in its proper perspective. During such moments you'll have to choose between emphasizing your skiers' development or winning. If your priorities are in order, your racers' well-being will take precedence over your team's record every time.

Take the following actions to better define your outlook:

1. Determine your priorities for the season.
2. Prepare for situations that challenge your priorities.
3. Set goals for yourself and your skiers that are consistent with those priorities.
4. Plan how you and your skiers can best attain those goals.
5. Review your goals frequently to be sure you are staying on track.

It is particularly important for coaches to give some individual attention to each and every one of their young athletes. Each youngster, regardless of potential, deserves the opportunity to develop skills—even if it means sacrificing some time spent with your most talented skiers.

Remember that the challenge and joy of sport is experienced through striving to win, not through winning itself. Ski racers who are ignored are less likely to take advantage of the opportunity to strive to win. And herein lies the irony: A coach who helps all of his or her skiers to develop skills will, in the end, come out on top.

ACEP has a motto that will help you keep your outlook in the best interest of the kids on your team. It summarizes in four words all you need to remember when establishing your coaching priorities:

Athletes First, Winning Second

This motto recognizes that striving to win is an important, even vital part of sport. But it emphatically states that no efforts in striving to win should be made at the expense of athletes' well-being, development, and enjoyment.

Affection

This is another important tool you will want to have in your coaching kit: a genuine concern for the young people you coach. *Affection* involves having a love for children, a desire to share with them your love and knowledge of sport, and the patience and understanding that allows each individual skiing for you to grow from his or her involvement in ski racing.

Successful coaches have a real concern for the health and welfare of their athletes. They care that each child on the team has an enjoyable and successful experience. They have a strong desire to work with children and be involved in their growth. And they have the patience to work with those who are slower to learn or less capable of performing. If you have such qualities or are willing to work hard to develop them, then you have the affection necessary to coach young athletes.

You can demonstrate your affection and patience many ways, including the following:

- Make an effort to get to know each skier on your team.
- Treat each skier as an individual.
- Empathize with skiers who are trying to learn new and difficult skills.
- Treat skiers as you would like to be treated under similar circumstances.
- Be in control of your emotions.

- Show your enthusiasm for being involved with your team.
- Keep an upbeat and positive tone in all of your communications.

Character

Youngsters learn by listening to what adults say. But they learn even more by watching the behaviors of certain important individuals. As a coach, you are likely to be a significant figure in the lives of your skiers. Will you be a good role model? Having good *character* means modeling appropriate behaviors for sport and life. That means more than just saying the right things. What you say and what you do must match. There is no place in coaching for the "Do as I say, not as I do" philosophy. Be in control before, during, and after all races and practices. And don't be afraid to admit that you were wrong. No one is perfect!

Consider the following steps to becoming a good role model:

- Evaluate your strengths and weaknesses.
- Build on your strengths.
- Set goals for yourself to improve upon those areas you would not like to see mimicked.
- If you slip up, apologize to your team and to yourself. You'll do better next time.

Humor

Humor is often overlooked as a coaching tool. For our use, it means having the ability to laugh at yourself and with your ski racers during practices and competitions. Nothing helps balance the tone of a serious, skill-learning session like a chuckle or two. And a sense of humor puts in perspective the many mistakes your young skiers will make. So don't get upset over each miscue or respond negatively to erring skiers. Allow your skiers

and yourself to enjoy the "ups," and don't dwell on the "downs."

Here are some tips for injecting humor into your practices:

- Make practices fun by including a variety of activities.
- Keep all skiers involved in drills and progressions.
- Consider laughter from your skiers a sign of enjoyment, not a lack of discipline.
- Smile!

Where Do You Stand?

Now evaluate your "coaching tool kit," and rank yourself on each of the three questions concerning the five coaching tools. Simply circle the number that best describes your present status on each item. Then total your score for each "tool."

Not at all		Somewhat		Very much so
1	2	3	4	5

Comprehension

1. Could you explain the rules of ski racing to parents without studying for a long time? — 1 2 3 4 5
2. Do you know how to organize and conduct safe ski racing practices? — 1 2 3 4 5
3. Do you know how to provide first aid for most common, minor skiing injuries? — 1 2 3 4 5

Comprehension Score: _____

Outlook

4. Do you keep winning in its proper perspective when you coach? — 1 2 3 4 5
5. Do you plan for every meeting, practice, and race? — 1 2 3 4 5
6. Do you have a vision of what your skiers will be able to do by the end of the season? — 1 2 3 4 5

Outlook Score: _____

Affection

7. Do you enjoy working with children? — 1 2 3 4 5
8. Are you patient with youngsters learning new skills? — 1 2 3 4 5
9. Are you able to show your skiers that you care? — 1 2 3 4 5

Affection Score: _____

Character

10. Are your words consistent with your behaviors? — 1 2 3 4 5
11. Are you a good model for your skiers? — 1 2 3 4 5
12. Do you keep negative emotions under control before, during, and after races? — 1 2 3 4 5

Character Score: _____

Humor

13. Do you usually smile at your skiers? — 1 2 3 4 5
14. Are your practices fun? — 1 2 3 4 5
15. Are you able to laugh at your mistakes? — 1 2 3 4 5

Humor Score: _____

If you scored 9 or less on any of the coaching tools, be sure to reread those sections of the unit carefully. And even if you scored 15 on each tool, don't be complacent. Keep learning! Then you'll be well equipped with the tools you need to coach young athletes.

How Should I Communicate With My Racers?

EVERYBODY GOT THAT?

N̲ow you know the tools needed to COACH: Comprehension, Outlook, Affection, Character, and Humor are essential for effective coaching. Without them, you'd have a difficult time getting started. But none of these tools will work if you don't know how to use them with your athletes—and that requires skillful *communication*.

This unit examines what communication is and how you can become a more effective communicator-coach.

What's Involved in Communication?

Coaches often believe that communication involves only instructing skiers to do something, but verbal direction is only one part of the communication process. More than half of what is communicated in a message is nonverbal. So remember when you are coaching that "actions speak louder than words."

Communication in its simplest form involves two people: a sender and a receiver. The sender can transmit the message verbally, through facial expression, and with body language. Once the message is sent, the receiver must try to determine the meaning of the message. A receiver who fails to attend or listen will miss part, if not all, of the message.

How Can I Send More Effective Messages?

Young athletes often have little understanding of the rules and skills of ski racing, and probably have less confidence in trying. So they need accurate, understandable, and supportive messages to help them along. That's why it's so important for you to send verbal and nonverbal messages effectively.

Verbal Messages

"Sticks and stones may break my bones, but words will never hurt me" isn't true. Spoken words can have a strong and long-lasting effect. And coaches' words are particularly influential, because youngsters place great importance on what coaches say. Therefore, whether you are correcting a misbehavior, teaching a skier how to plant a ski pole, or praising a skier for good effort,

- *be positive, but honest;*
- *state it clearly and simply;*
- *say it loud enough and say it again; and*
- *send consistent messages.*

Be Positive, But Honest

Nothing turns people off more than hearing someone nag all the time. Young athletes are similarly discouraged by a coach who gripes

constantly. The kids on your team need encouragement, because many of them doubt their ability to ski race. So look for and tell your skiers what they do well.

On the other hand, don't cover up poor or incorrect execution with rosy words of praise. Kids know all too well when they've made a mistake, and no cheerfully expressed cliché can undo their errors. And, if you fail to acknowledge racers' errors, your athletes will think you are a phony.

State It Clearly and Simply

Positive and honest messages are good, but only if expressed directly and in words your skiers can understand. "Beating around the bush" is an ineffective and inefficient way to send messages verbally. If you ramble, your ski racers will miss the point of your message and probably lose interest. Here are some tips for saying things clearly.

- Organize your thoughts before speaking to your athletes.
- Explain things thoroughly, but don't bore them with long-winded monologues.
- Use language that your skiers can understand, but avoid trying to be "hip" by using their slang.

Say It Loud Enough and Say It Again

Talk to your team in a voice that all members can hear and interpret. It's okay, in fact appropriate, to soften your voice when speaking to a skier about an individual problem. But when your message is for all your racers to hear, make sure they can! A word of caution, however: Don't dominate the setting with a booming voice that distracts your athletes' attention from their performances.

Sometimes what you say, even if stated loud and clear, won't sink in the first time. This may be particularly true with young athletes hearing words they don't fully understand. To avoid boring repetition but still get your message across, say the same thing in a slightly different way. For instance, you might first tell your skiers, "Get your weight forward." Then, soon thereafter, remind them, "Keep your arms up in front to maintain better balance." The second message may

Compliment Sandwich

A good way to handle situations in which you have identified and must correct improper technique is to serve your skiers a "compliment sandwich."

1. Point out what the athlete did correctly.
2. Let the skier know what was incorrect in the performance and instruct him or her how to correct it.
3. Encourage the skier by reemphasizing what he or she did well.

get through to some skiers who missed it at first.

Send Consistent Messages

People often say things in a way that implies a different message. For example, a touch of sarcasm added to the words "way to go" sends an entirely different message than the words themselves suggest. It is essential that you avoid sending such mixed messages. Keep the tone of your voice consistent with the words you use. And don't say something one day and contradict it the next; your athletes will get confused.

Nonverbal Messages

Just as you should be consistent in the tone of voice and words you use, you should also keep your verbal and nonverbal messages consistent. An extreme example of failing to do this would be shaking your head, indicating disapproval, while at the same time telling a skier "nice try." Which is the skier to believe, your gesture or your words? Messages can be sent nonverbally in a number of ways. Facial expressions and body language are just two of the more obvious forms of nonverbal signals that can help you when you coach.

Facial Expressions

The look on a person's face is the quickest clue to what he or she thinks or feels. Your skiers know this, so they will study your face, looking for any sign that will tell them more than the words you say. Don't try to fool them by putting on a happy or blank "mask." They'll see through it, and you'll lose credibility.

Stone-faced expressions are no help to kids who need cues as to how they are performing. They will just assume you're unhappy or disinterested. So don't be afraid to smile. A smile from a coach can boost the confidence of an unsure young athlete. Plus, a smile lets your ski racers know that you are happy coaching them. But don't overdo it, because your skiers won't be able to tell when you are genuinely pleased by something they've done or when you are just "putting on" a smiling face.

Body Language

How would your skiers think you felt if you came to practice slouched over, with head down and shoulders slumped? Tired? Bored? Unhappy? How would they think you felt if you watched them during a race with your hands on your hips, jaws clenched, and face red? Upset with them? Disgusted with an official's decision? Probably some or all of these things would enter your skiers' minds. That's why you should carry yourself in a pleasant, confident, and vigorous manner. Such a posture not only projects happiness with your coaching role, but it also provides a good example for your young racers who may model your behavior.

Physical contact can also be a very important use of body language. A handshake, a pat on the back, an arm around the shoulder, or even a big hug are effective ways of showing approval, concern, affection, and joy to your skiers. Youngsters are especially in need of this type of nonverbal message. Keep within the obvious moral and legal limits, but don't be reluctant to touch your skiers and send a message that is truly best expressed only in that way.

How Can I Improve My Receiving Skills?

Now let's examine the other half of the communication process—receiving messages. Too often people are very good senders yet very poor receivers of messages; they seem to naturally enjoy hearing themselves talk more than listening to others. As a coach of young athletes, it is essential that you receive their verbal and nonverbal messages effectively. You can be a better receiver if you are willing to read about the keys to receiving messages and then make a strong effort to use them with your ski racers. You'll be surprised at what you've been missing.

Attention!

First, you must pay attention; you must want to hear what others have to communicate to you. That's not always easy when you're busy coaching and have many things competing for your attention. But in one-to-one or team meetings with skiers, you must really focus on what they are telling you, both verbally and nonverbally. Not only will such focused attention help you catch every word they say, but you'll also notice their moods and physical states, and you'll get an idea of their feelings toward you and other racers on the team.

Listen CARE-FULLY

How we receive messages from others, perhaps more than anything else we do, demonstrates how much we care for the sender and what that person has to tell us. If you care

little for your skiers or have little regard for what they have to say, it will show in how you attend and listen to them.

Check yourself. While one of your skiers is talking to you, do you find your mind wandering to what you are going to do after practice? Do you frequently have to ask your skiers, "What did you say?" If so, you need to work on your attending and listening skills. If you find that you're missing the messages your athletes send, perhaps the most critical question you should ask yourself is this: Do I care?

How Do I Put It All Together?

So far we've discussed separately the sending and receiving of messages. But we all know that senders and receivers switch roles several times during an interaction. One person initiates a communication by sending a message to another person, who then receives the message. The receiver then switches roles and becomes the sender by responding to the person who sent the initial message. These verbal and nonverbal responses are called feedback.

Your racers will be looking to you for feedback all the time. They will want to know how you think they are performing, what you think of their ideas, and whether their efforts please you. How you respond will strongly affect your athletes. So let's take a look at a few general types of feedback and examine their possible effects.

Providing Instructions

With young skiers, much of your feedback will involve answering questions about how to perform skiing skills. Your instructive responses to these questions should include both verbal and nonverbal feedback. The following are suggestions for giving instructional feedback:

- Keep verbal instructions simple and concise.
- Use demonstrations or videotape training to provide nonverbal instructional feedback (see Unit 4).
- Walk skiers through the skill, or use a slow-motion demonstration if they are having trouble learning.

Correcting Errors

When your skiers perform incorrectly, you need to provide informative feedback to correct the error—and the sooner the better. And when you do correct errors, keep in mind these three principles: Use negative criticism sparingly, correct only one error at a time, and keep calm.

Use Negative Criticism Sparingly

Although you may need to punish skiers for horseplay or dangerous activities by scolding them or temporarily removing them from activity, avoid reprimanding skiers for performance errors. Punishing athletes for honest mistakes makes them afraid to even try; nothing ruins a youngster's enjoyment of a sport more than a coach who harps on every miscue. So instead, correct your skiers by using the positive approach. They'll enjoy skiing more and you'll enjoy coaching more.

Correct One Error at a Time

Given that ski racing is a dynamic sport with varying terrain, snow conditions, courses, and more, you will see your skiers make a lot of errors. Inexperienced ski coaches will want to point out every error they see. You must resist the urge to immediately correct every error. Instead, focus only on one. The one you choose should relate to the day's tasks, or be one your skier seems to make fairly frequently. Correcting every error you see will keep your skiers too focused on mistakes, and not on what they are trying to do.

Keep Calm

Don't fly off the handle when your skiers make mistakes. Remember, you're coaching young and inexperienced ski racers, not elite athletes. You'll therefore see more incorrect than correct technique, and you'll probably have more discipline problems than you expect. But throwing a tantrum over each error or misbehavior will only inhibit skiers or suggest to them the wrong kind of behavior to model. Let your skiers know that mistakes aren't the end of the world, and keep your composure!

Positive Feedback

Praising ski racers when they have performed or behaved well is an effective way to get them to repeat (or try to repeat) that behavior in the future. And positive feedback for effort is an especially effective way to motivate youngsters to work on difficult skills. So rather than shouting and providing negative feedback to a skier who has made a mistake, try offering a compliment sandwich, described on page 13.

Sometimes just the way you word feedback can make it more positive than negative. For example, instead of saying, "Don't aim straight at the gate," you might say, "Try to complete most of your turn by the time you get to the gate." Then your skiers will be focusing on what to do instead of what not to do.

You can give positive feedback verbally and nonverbally. Telling a ski racer, especially in front of teammates, that he or she has performed well is a great way to increase a kid's confidence. And a pat on the back or a handshake can be a very tangible way of communicating your recognition of a skier's performance.

Coaches, be positive!

Only a very small percentage of ACEP-trained coaches' behaviors are negative.

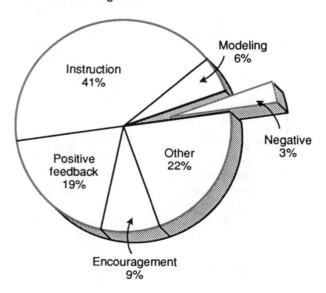

Who Else Do I Need to Communicate With?

Coaching not only involves sending and receiving messages and providing proper feedback to players, it also includes interacting with skiers' parents, race officials, ski area operators, and other coaches. If you don't communicate effectively with these groups of people, your coaching career could be unpleasant and short-lived. So try these suggestions for communicating with each group.

Parents

A skier's parents need to be assured that their son or daughter is under the direction of a coach who is both knowledgeable about ski racing and concerned about the youngster's well-being. You can put their worries to rest by holding a preseason parent orientation meeting in which you describe your background and your approach to coaching. If parents contact you with a concern during the season, listen to them closely and try to offer positive responses. If you need to communicate with parents, catch them after a practice, give them a phone call, or send a note through the mail. Messages sent to parents through children are too often lost, misinterpreted, or forgotten.

Race Officials

How you communicate with officials will have a great influence on the way your skiers behave toward them. Therefore, you need to set the tone. Greet officials with a handshake, an introduction, and perhaps some casual conversation about the upcoming race. Indicate your respect for them before, during, and after the contest. Keep in mind that most ski racing officials are volunteers. So don't make nasty remarks, shout, or use disrespectful body gestures. Your skiers will see you do it, and they'll get the idea that such behavior is appropriate. Plus, if the official hears or sees you, the communication between the two of you will break down.

In short, you take care of the coaching, and let the officials take care of the officiating.

Ski Area Operators

Having access to a good slope for training requires the permission and cooperation of ski area management. It is important for you to develop a good rapport with them. Coordinating when your team can use the hill to train and working together on safety issues are two key cooperative decisions that must be made. Your relationship with the management at your ski area is vital to the overall success of your program. See Unit 6 for more information.

Other Coaches

At ski races, most coaches enjoy the opportunity to visit with coaches. Consider working with another coach to set a morning warm-up course for your teams. Perhaps two of you can help out each other's skiers during the race. During the competition, don't get into a personal feud with the opposing coach. Remember, it's the kids, not the coaches, who are competing.

Summary Checklist

Now, check your coaching communication skills by answering yes or no to the following questions.

	Yes	No
1. Are your verbal messages to your skiers positive and honest?	___	___
2. Do you speak loudly, clearly, and with vocabulary your athletes understand?	___	___
3. Do you remember to repeat instructions to your skiers, in case they didn't understand you the first time?	___	___
4. Are your tone of voice and nonverbal messages consistent with the words you use?	___	___
5. Do your facial expressions and body language express interest in and happiness with your coaching role?	___	___
6. Are you attentive to your skiers and able to pick up even their small verbal and nonverbal cues?	___	___
7. Do you really care about what your athletes say to you?	___	___
8. Do you instruct rather than criticize when your skiers make errors?	___	___
9. Are you usually positive when responding to things your athletes say and do?	___	___
10. Do you try to communicate in a cooperative, respectful manner with skiers' parents, race officials, ski area operators, and other coaches?	___	___

If you answered no to any of these questions, you may want to refer back to the section of the unit where the topic was discussed. Now is the time to address communication problems, not when you're coaching your skiers.

UNIT 4

How Do I Get My Team Ready to Race?

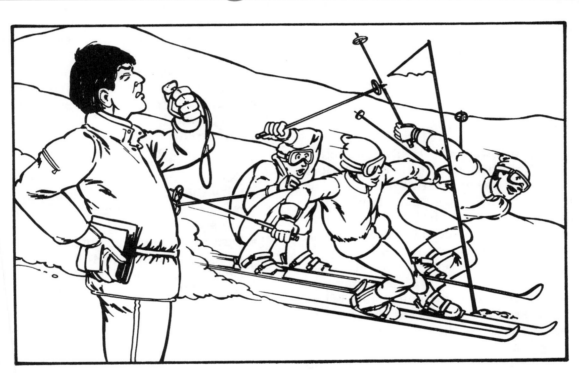

To coach alpine ski racing, you must understand its basic rules, skills, and specific teaching progressions for both skiing and racing. The second part of this *Rookie Coaches Ski Racing Guide* provides the basic information you'll need to understand the sport.

But all the ski racing knowledge in the world will do you little good unless you present it effectively to your skiers. That's

why this unit is so important. In it you will learn the steps to take in teaching sport skills, as well as practical guidelines for planning your season and individual practices.

How Do I Teach Sport Skills?

Many people believe that the only qualification needed to coach is to have ski raced. It's helpful to have raced, but there is much more to successful coaching. And even if you haven't ski raced, you can still teach the skills of the sport effectively using this IDEA:

I — Introduce the skill.
D — Demonstrate the skill.
E — Explain the skill.
A — Attend to skiers practicing the skill.

Introduce the Skill

Ski racers, especially young and inexperienced ones, need to know what skill they are learning and why they are learning it. You should therefore take these three steps every time you introduce a skill to your skiers:

1. Get your skiers' attention.
2. Name the skill.
3. Explain the importance of the skill.

Get Your Skiers' Attention

Because youngsters are easily distracted, use some method to get their attention. Some coaches use interesting news items or stories. Others use jokes. And others simply project an enthusiasm that gets their skiers to listen. Whatever method you use, speak slightly above normal volume and look your skiers in the eye when you speak. Also, position your skiers so that all of them are safely away from any oncoming skier traffic and so that they can see and hear you. Arrange the skiers so they are facing you and not some source of distraction. Then ask if everyone can see and hear you before you begin.

Name the Skill

Although you might mention other common names for the skill, decide which one you'll use and stick with it. This will help avoid confusion and enhance communication with your skiers.

Explain the Importance of the Skill

Although the importance of a skill may be apparent to you, your skiers may be less able to see how it will help them become better ski racers. Offer them a reason for learning the skill and describe how it relates to becoming a faster skier.

The most difficult aspect of coaching is this: Coaches must learn to let athletes learn. Sport skills should be taught so they have meaning to the child, not just meaning to the coach.

Rainer Martens, ACEP Founder

Demonstrate the Skill

The demonstration step is the most important part of teaching skiing skills to young racers who may have never done anything that closely resembles the skill. They need a picture, not just words. They need to see how the skill is performed.

If you are unable to perform the skill correctly, have an assistant coach or another competent skier perform the demonstration. These tips will help make your demonstrations more effective:

- Use correct form.
- Demonstrate the skill several times.
- Slow the skill down, if possible, during one or two performances so skiers can see every movement involved.
- Perform the skill at different angles so your skiers can get a full view of it.
- Demonstrate the skill from above, next to, and below where your skiers are watching.
- If necessary, break the skill down into smaller parts or learning sequences.

Explain the Skill

Skiers learn more effectively if they're given a brief explanation of the skill along with the demonstration. Use simple terms to describe the skill, and if possible, relate it to ones they've previously learned. Ask your skiers if they understand your description. If one of them looks confused, have him or her explain the skill back to you. Complex skills often are better understood if they are explained in more manageable parts. For instance, if you want to teach your skiers how to ski parallel turns, you might take the following steps:

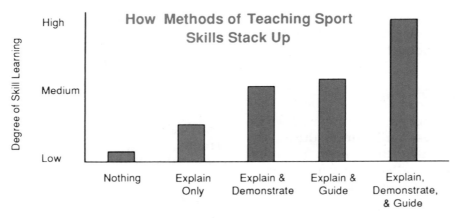

How Methods of Teaching Sport Skills Stack Up

Degree of Skill Learning — High / Medium / Low

Coach Teaching Method — Nothing / Explain Only / Explain & Demonstrate / Explain & Guide / Explain, Demonstrate, & Guide

1. Show a correct performance of the entire skill and explain its function in ski racing.
2. Break down the skill and point out its components.
3. Have skiers perform each of the component skills you have already taught them: balancing, steering, edging, turn completion, weight transfer.
4. After skiers have demonstrated their ability to perform the separate parts of the skill in sequence, reexplain the entire skill.
5. Have them practice the skill.

Attend to Skiers Practicing the Skill

If the skill you selected was within your skiers' capabilities and you have done an effective job of introducing, demonstrating, and explaining it, your skiers should be ready to try it. Some skiers may need to be physically guided through the movements during their first few attempts at the skill. For example, some skiers may need your hands-on help to find a balanced, athletic position on their skis. Walking unsure athletes through the skill in this way will help them gain confidence to perform the skill on their own.

Your teaching duties don't end when all your athletes have demonstrated that they understand how to perform the skill. In fact, a significant part of your teaching will involve observing closely your skiers' hit-and-miss trial performances. As you observe skiers' efforts in drills and activities, offer positive,

corrective feedback in the form of the "compliment sandwich" described in Unit 3. If a skier performs the skill properly, acknowledge it and offer praise. Keep in mind that your feedback will have a great influence on your skiers' motivation to practice and improve their performance.

Remember too that young skiers need individual instruction. So set aside a time before, during, or after practice to give individual help.

What Planning Do I Need to Do?

Beginning coaches often make the mistake of showing up for the first practice with no particular plan in mind. These coaches find that their practices are unorganized, their skiers are frustrated and inattentive, and the amount and quality of their skill instruction is limited. Planning is essential to successful teaching and coaching. And it doesn't begin on the way to practice!

Preseason Planning

Effective coaches begin planning well before the start of the season. Planning during the preseason can make the year more enjoyable, successful, and safe for you and your skiers if you do the following:

- Familiarize yourself with the United States Ski Association, especially its philosophy and goals regarding junior skiing.
- Examine the availability of facilities, equipment, instructional aids, and other materials needed for practices and competitions.
- Make sure to see if you have liability insurance to cover you when one of your skiers is hurt (see Unit 5). If you don't have coverage, get some.
- Establish your coaching priorities regarding having fun, developing skiers' skills, and winning.
- Meet with the coaching staff for your team to discuss the philosophy, goals, team rules, and plans for the season.
- Register skiers for the team. Have them complete a skier information form and obtain medical clearance forms, if required.
- Institute an injury-prevention program for your skiers. With your local ski patrol, plan how to handle injuries should they occur.
- Hold a parent orientation meeting to inform parents of your background, philosophy, goals, and instructional approach. Also, give a brief overview of the ski racing rules, terms, and strategies to familiarize parents or guardians with the sport.

You may be surprised at the number of things you should do even before the first practice. But if you address these items during the preseason, the season will be much more enjoyable and productive for you and your ski racers.

In-Season Planning

Activities during the season should reflect choices that will help your skiers develop physical and mental skills, knowledge of rules, ability to be a good sport, and love for ski racing. All of these goals are important, but we'll focus on the skills and tactics of ski racing to give you an idea of how to itemize your objectives.

Goal Setting

What you plan to do during the season must be reasonable for the maturity and skill level of your ski racers. In terms of ski racing skills and tactics, you should teach young skiers the fundamentals and move on to more complex activities only after they have mastered these basics.

To begin the season, you might set your skiers' instructional goals to include the following:

My skiers will

- maintain balance throughout the turn,
- steer the skis into the turn,
- edge cleanly throughout the turn,
- pressure the outside ski throughout the turn,
- maintain control while linking several turns together,
- be adaptable to a variety of snow conditions and terrains,
- understand the basic tactics of timing and line,
- consistently look ahead while in the race course,
- demonstrate an ability to inspect race courses on their own, and
- demonstrate knowledge of ski racing rules.

Organizing

After you've defined the skills and tactics you want your skiers to learn during the season, you can plan how to teach them in practices. But be flexible! If your skiers are having difficulty learning a skill or tactic, take some extra time until they get the hang of it—even if that means moving back your schedule.

After all, if your skiers are unable to perform the fundamental skills, they'll never execute the more complex skills you have scheduled for them.

Still, it helps to have a plan for progressing skiers through skills during the season. The slalom and giant slalom skill progressions in Unit 8 will show how to schedule your skill and strategy instruction in an organized and progressive manner. Also, Unit 7 has an excellent teaching progression for basic skills that you will find quite helpful for even your youngest skiers. If this is your first coaching experience, you may follow the progression as it is presented. If you have some previous experience, you may want to modify the schedule to better fit the needs of your athletes.

What Makes Up a Good Practice?

A good instructional plan makes preparing for practice much easier. Have skiers work on the most basic skills on gentle terrain in early-season practice sessions. And make sure that skiers master basic skills before moving on to more advanced ones, or on to more challenging terrain.

It is helpful to establish one objective for each practice, but try to include a variety of activities related to that objective. For example, although your primary objective might be to improve your skiers' slalom turns, you should have skiers perform several different drills designed to enhance that single skill. To add further variety to your practices, vary the order of the activities you schedule for skiers to perform. In general, we recommend that each of your practices include the following:

- *Warm up*
- *Practice previously taught skills*
- *Teach and practice new skills*
- *Practice under competitive conditions*
- *Cool down*
- *Evaluate*

Warm Up

Before going out in the cold, your skiers should be preparing their bodies for vigorous activity. If space allows, a 5- to 10-minute period indoors consisting of a few easy exercises, followed by stretching, is a good start. This, followed by skiing a few controlled runs on moderate terrain and stretching on skis, should be sufficient for youngsters to limber up their muscles and reduce the risk of injury.

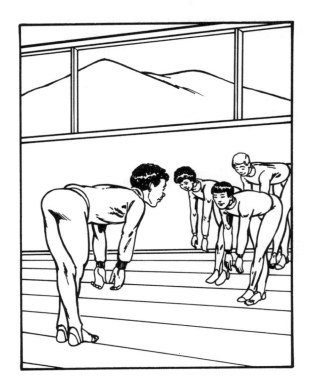

Practice Previously Taught Skills

Devote part of each practice to working on the fundamental skills your skiers already know. But remember, kids like variety. So organize and modify drills to keep everyone involved and interested. Praise and encourage skiers when you notice improvement, and offer individual assistance to those who need help.

Teach and Practice New Skills

Build on your skiers' existing skills by giving them something new to practice each session. The proper method for teaching sport skills is described on pages 19 to 21. Refer to those pages if you have any questions about teaching new skills or if you want to evaluate your teaching approach periodically during the season.

Practice Under Competitive Conditions

Competition among teammates during practices prepares skiers for actual races and informs young athletes about their abilities relative to those of their peers. Youngsters also seem to have more fun in competitive activities.

You can create racelike conditions by using competitive drills, contests, and head-to-head courses (see Units 7 and 8). However, consider the following guidelines before introducing competition into your practices.

- Match skiers by ability and physical maturity.
- Make sure that skiers can execute fundamental skills before they compete.
- Emphasize performing well, not winning, in every competition.
- Give skiers room to make mistakes by avoiding constant evaluation of their performances.

Cool Down

Each practice should wind down with kids skiing a few easy runs, and then stretching indoors afterward. The cool-down allows athletes' bodies to return to the resting state and avoid stiffness, and it affords you an opportunity to review the practice.

Evaluate

At the end of practice, spend a few minutes with your skiers reviewing how well the session accomplished the objectives you had set. This is an excellent opportunity to reinforce positive outcomes of the practice and keep your skiers focused on their improvements.

How Do I Put a Practice Together?

Simply knowing the six practice components is not enough. You must also be able to arrange those components into a logical progression and fit them into a time schedule. Now, using your instructional goals as a guide for selecting what skills to have your skiers work on, try to plan a ski racing practice session you might conduct. The following example should help you get started.

Summary Checklist

During your season, check your planning and teaching skills periodically. As you gain more coaching experience, you should be able to answer yes to each of the following questions.

When you plan, do you remember to plan for

____ preseason events like skier registration, liability protection, use of facilities, and parent orientation?

____ season goals such as the development of skiers' physical skills, mental skills, sportsmanship, and enjoyment?

____ practice components such as warm-up, practicing previously taught skills, teaching and practicing new skills, practicing under competitive conditions, cool-down, and evaluation?

When you teach skiing skills to your ski racers, do you

____ arrange the skiers so all can see and hear?

____ introduce the skill clearly and explain its importance?

____ demonstrate the skill properly several times?

____ explain the skill simply and accurately?

____ attend closely to skiers practicing the skill?

____ offer corrective, positive feedback or praise after observing skiers' attempts at the skill?

Sample Practice Plan

Performance Objective. Skiers will be able to plant their poles between each turn to help timing.

Component	Time	Activity or drill
Warm up	10 min 2 runs	Indoor: stretching On-snow: Easy runs, stretching
Practice previously taught skills	1 run	Quiet upper body Arms up in front
Teach and practice	3 runs	Pole plants
Competition conditions	1 run	Pair up; see who can make the most slalom turns with pole plants in 50 yards
Cool down and evaluate	2 runs	Easy turning on a gentle slope Stretching

Each ski area is different. For small ski areas like those found in the Midwest, you may want to double the number of runs listed in the practice plans.

UNIT 5

What About Safety?

One of your skiers crosses the finish line, ending a blistering run. After glancing at the scoreboard, you turn toward your racer. You see she has fallen in the finish area and is not getting up. What do you do?

One of the least pleasant aspects of coaching is seeing athletes get hurt. Fortunately, there are many preventive measures coaches can institute to reduce the risk. But in spite of such efforts, injury remains a reality of sport participation. Consequently, you must be prepared to provide first aid when injuries occur and to protect yourself against unjustified lawsuits. This unit describes how you can

- create the safest possible environment for your skiers,
- provide emergency first aid to skiers when they get hurt, and
- protect yourself from injury liability.

How Do I Keep My Skiers From Getting Hurt?

Injuries may occur because of poor preventive measures. Part of your planning, described in Unit 4, should include steps that give your skiers the best possible chance for injury-free participation. These steps include the following:

- *Preseason physical examination*
- *Physical conditioning*
- *Proper ski equipment*
- *Appropriate training site*
- *Matching skiers to appropriate terrain, skill, and competitive levels*
- *Warning of inherent risks*
- *Proper supervision and record keeping*
- *Warm-up and cool-down*

Preseason Physical Examination

Even in the absence of severe injury or ongoing illness, your skiers should have a physical exam every 2 years. Any skier with a known medical condition or preexisting injury should have a physician's consent before being allowed to participate. You should also have each skier's parents or guardians sign a participation agreement form and a release form to allow their son or daughter to be treated in the case of a medical emergency.

Physical Conditioning

Muscles, tendons, and ligaments unaccustomed to vigorous and long-lasting physical activity are prone to injury. Therefore, prepare your athletes to withstand the exertion of ski racing. An effective conditioning program includes the components of flexibility, endurance, strength and power, agility, and balance. Use games when you can to keep players from getting bored or viewing the activity as work. Playing a wide variety of sports is a good way for young kids to prepare for skiing.

Proper Ski Equipment

It is important that skiers' skis, boots, and bindings be appropriate for their height, weight, and ability level. Binding settings should be set and periodically checked by a trained coach or ski shop technician.

Informed Consent Form

I hereby give my permission for _____ to participate in

_____ during the athletic season beginning in 199____. Further, I authorize the school to provide emergency treatment of an injury to or illness of my child if qualified medical personnel consider treatment necessary *and* perform the treatment. This authorization is granted only if I cannot be reached and a reasonable effort has been made to do so.

Date _____ Parent or guardian _____

Address _____ Phone ( ) _____

Family physician _____ Phone ( ) _____

Preexisting medical conditions (e.g., allergies or chronic illnesses) _____

_____

Other(s) to also contact in case of emergency _____

Relationship to child _____ Phone ( ) _____

My child and I are aware that participating in _____ is a potentially hazardous activity. I assume all risks associated with participation in this sport, including but not limited to falls, contact with other participants, the effects of the weather, traffic, and other reasonable risk conditions associated with the sport. All such risks to my child are known and understood by me.

I understand this informed consent form and agree to its conditions on behalf of my child.

Child's signature _____ Date _____

Parent's signature _____ Date _____

Warm, layered clothing, including a water-proof layer, is a must for all skiers, coaches and competitors alike. To keep vision clear and protect the eyes, racers should always wear goggles when running gates; for free-skiing, either goggles or unbreakable sun-glasses are advisable. Helmets are manda-tory for downhill and super-g competitions and optional for other events. It is important that you require helmets whenever skiers are practicing any elements of the speed events. See Unit 6 for more information on ski equip-ment.

Appropriate Training Site

Where your skiers practice and race is an important factor for safety. Common sense and awareness are the watchwords for a safe and healthy environment. The slope should not be too steep or rough for your skiers' abilities. The terrain you select should be dictated by the needs of your weaker skiers. Work with managers of the ski area to make sure your practice area is closed to, or sepa-rated from, public skiers.

Look for the fall line of the slope (the direction a ball would travel if it rolled down the hill). That is where your skiers will most likely end up if they fall. The slope where you set courses for skiers should have plenty of room on each side and below to allow skiers to fall and recover safely. It's not practical or feasible to fence off every tree or potential obstacle along the side of the trail, but pru-dent use of fencing is advised in narrow or more hazardous areas. Work with the area's ski patrol to determine what makes sense for safety; make sure they know when and where your practices take place. See Unit 6 for guidelines for setting a safe course.

Finally, you as the coach should always be aware of the broader safety picture. Watch for changing snow and weather conditions in your area, and always be alert to potentially dangerous situations. Make sure your skiers have adequate clothing for the conditions and that their equipment is in proper work-ing order.

Matching Skiers to Appropriate Terrain, Skill, and Competition Levels

It is your responsibility to know your ath-letes and understand their limitations. A steep, bumpy, icy slope or a long, fast race course might be the perfect setting for the experienced, gifted ski racer. But for novices, it can be an intimidating and possibly dan-gerous situation. There is a fine line between challenging your athletes and getting them in over their heads. When in doubt, err on the side of safety and caution. Your athletes will

trust you to provide a situation where they can go all out and yet be in control and stay within their limits.

You should evaluate each skier before participation to determine his or her individual level of proficiency. For safety, it is critical that you teach each skier the skills and progressions appropriate to his or her level. Novice ski racers participate in local, recreational-type events. As they progress in ski racing, they move on to Junior Olympic and age-group competition. Only a few make it to elite levels of ski racing. Be sure that what you ask of your skiers is within their abilities and experience. It will be safer and, not coincidentally, more fun for your kids.

Warning of Inherent Risks

All athletic activities involve certain inherent risks, and ski racing is no exception. Even under the best of conditions, injuries can and do occur, and because ski racing involves speed over uneven terrain, the potential risks include serious, catastrophic injury and even death.

Make sure your athletes know, understand, and heed your warnings of the known risks of participating in ski racing. Repeat these warnings regularly and include safety tips in each session.

A preseason parent orientation meeting is a good opportunity to explain the risks of skiing to parents and participants. It is also a good time to have both participants and their parents sign waivers releasing you from liability should an injury occur. Such documents do not relieve you of responsibility for your skiers' well-being, but they are recommended by many lawyers, because they are proof that parents and ski racers have been warned about risks.

Proper Supervision and Record Keeping

With youngsters, your mere presence on the practice hill is not enough; you must actively plan and direct team activities and closely observe and evaluate skiers' participation and energy levels. You're the watchdog responsible for their welfare. So if you notice a skier favoring one leg or grimacing, give her or him a rest and examine the extent of the injury.

As a coach, you're also required to enforce the rules of the sport, prohibit horseplay, and hold practices only under safe conditions. These specific supervisory activities will make the practice environment safer for your skiers and help protect you from liability in the event of an injury.

For further protection, keep records of your season plans, practice plans, and skiers' injuries. Season and practice plans come in handy when you need evidence that skiers have been taught certain skills, and accurate, detailed accident-report forms offer protection against unfounded lawsuits. Ask for these forms from the organization to which you belong. And hold onto these records for several years so that a former racer's "old skiing injury" doesn't come back to haunt you.

Warm-Up and Cool-Down

Although young bodies are generally very limber, they too can get tight from inactivity. Therefore, a warm-up period of approximately 10 minutes before each practice is strongly recommended. Warm-up should address each muscle group and get the heart rate elevated in preparation for strenuous activity. Easy running followed by stretching activities is a common sequence that skiers should try to do before coming out on the hill. An on-snow warm-up of easy skiing and stretching will prepare muscles for skiing.

As practice is winding down, slow athletes' heart rates. Then allow for a 5- to 10-minute period of easy stretching at the end of practice to help skiers avoid stiff muscles. You might end practice with some easy freeskiing, followed by stretching indoors and a verbal evaluation of the practice with your skiers.

What If One of My Skiers Gets Hurt?

No matter how comprehensive your prevention program is, injuries will occur. And when an injury does strike, chances are you will be the one in charge. The severity and nature of the injury will determine how actively involved you'll be in treating it. But regardless of how seriously a skier is hurt, it is your responsibility to know what steps to take. So let's look at how you can provide basic emergency care to your injured athletes.

Skiers injured on the slopes face two potential dangers: approaching skiers skiing into them and the cold environment. Because of this, always follow two steps when one of your skiers appears to be injured:

1. Protect the injured athlete from any approaching skiers by making sure that approaching skiers are aware of the injury, slow down, and avoid the area. Have another coach monitor skier traffic while you attend to your athlete. If the injury occurs while running gates, stop training until the injured skier is removed from the scene.

2. Keep the injured skier warm while waiting for the ski patrol to arrive. Remember, the injured skier will be lying directly on the snow, so extra care must be taken to maintain warmth. Use your own and others' parkas to cover the skier.

In addition to these two steps, you'll want to provide care for the specific situations outlined next.

Minor Injuries

Although no injury seems minor to the person experiencing it, most injuries are neither life-threatening nor severe enough to restrict participation. When injuries occur, take an active role in their initial treatment.

Sprains and Strains

The physical demands of ski racing often result in injury to the muscles or tendons (strains) or to the ligaments (sprains). When a skier suffers minor strains or sprains, immediately apply the PRICE method of injury care.

Bumps and Bruises

Inevitably, skiers make contact with gates and with snow or ice. If the force on a body part at impact is great enough, a bump or bruise will result. Shin bruises along the front of the boot are a common skiing injury. Many skiers will continue racing with such sore spots. But if the bump or bruise is large

---

The PRICE Method

P — Protect the athlete and injured body part from danger or further trauma.

R — Rest the area to avoid further damage and foster healing.

I — Ice the area to reduce swelling and pain.

C — Compress the area by securing an ice bag in place with an elastic wrap.

E — Elevate the injury above heart level to keep the blood from pooling in the area.

and painful, you should take appropriate action. Use the PRICE formula for injury care and monitor the injury. If swelling, discoloration, and pain have lessened, the skier may resume participation with protective padding; if not, the skier should be examined by a physician.

Serious Injuries

Head, neck, and back injuries, fractures, and injuries that cause a skier to lose consciousness are injuries that you cannot and should not try to treat yourself. But you should plan what you'll do if such an injury occurs. Your plan should include the following guidelines for action:

- Make prior arrangements with your area's ski patrol regarding procedures for handling injuries. They should always know when and where your practices will be held.
- Maintain the phone numbers and ensure the availability of nearby emergency care units.
- Assign an assistant coach or another adult the responsibility of contacting emergency medical help at your request.
- Do not move the injured athlete. Clearly mark the area above the athlete to signal skiers coming down the hill to avoid the area.
- Calm the injured athlete and keep others away from him or her. Keep the skier warm.
- Evaluate whether the athlete's breathing is stopped or irregular, and if necessary clear the airway with your fingers.
- If breathing has stopped, administer artificial respiration.
- If the athlete's heart has stopped, have a trained individual administer cardiopulmonary resuscitation (CPR).
- Remain with the athlete until medical personnel arrive.

Cold Emergencies

Because ski racing is a winter sport, you must always be aware of weather conditions and how they may affect your skiers. In extreme weather, you must make a judgment call as to whether or not to ski. When it is either extremely cold or wet, you may still decide to ski, but keep in mind these precautionary measures:

- Keep practice short, and keep skiers moving!
- Make sure there is a warm building nearby, where skiers can go to warm up.
- Make sure skiers are adequately dressed.
- Monitor skiers closely for signs of frostbite or hypothermia.

Frostbite

You are most likely to see signs of frostbite when temperatures are extremely cold, especially if the wind is blowing. Skiers are most likely to experience frostbite on their faces, fingers, and toes. At first the affected area will feel cold, then as frostbite sets in, it will feel numb.

Frostbite is the actual freezing of body tissue. The skin will appear white and waxy and feel stiff to the touch. Frostbite most commonly occurs on earlobes, the tip of the nose, and on cheeks just below the goggles. If you see frostbite, take the following action immediately:

- Have your skier cover the spot with a gloved hand and get inside a warm building immediately.
- Rapidly rewarm the affected area. One of the best ways is to take your own hand out of your glove and cover the frostbitten area with your warm hand. If toes are frostbitten, take off cold ski boots, then cover the area with warm hands.
- DO NOT RUB! The frostbitten area can be permanently damaged by rubbing.

You can't, of course, see frostbite on the fingers and toes when skiers are all bundled up. Be sure they are aware of the signs and symptoms of frostbite and know enough to go inside if their fingers or toes feel numb. Use a buddy system on really cold days so your skiers can check each others' faces every run.

If recognized early, frostbite causes little damage. However, if an area stays frozen for a long time, afterward it may blister, swell, or turn black. In that situation, a physician should be consulted.

Hypothermia

A potentially more dangerous situation is hypothermia—a loss of core body temperature. Temperatures don't have to be excessively cold for a skier to become hypothermic. Wet or windy weather, especially if skiers are inappropriately dressed, is when hypothermia is most likely to develop. Anyone can get hypothermia, but smaller people and females are likely to be affected first.

Symptoms of hypothermia are shivering, stiff and rigid muscles, and confusion. If left untreated, hypothermia can progress to unconsciousness and even death. Most likely, however, you will see it in its earliest stages and will be able to take steps to effectively treat it. Do the following if you suspect that one of your skiers is becoming hypothermic:

- Get the skier indoors immediately.
- Remove wet or cold clothing.
- Provide a heat source. Place the skier close to a fireplace or heater, and have warmer teammates snuggle up close.
- If your skier doesn't seem to be responding, contact the ski patrol.

How Do I Protect Myself?

When one of your skiers is injured, naturally your first concern is her or his well-being. Your feelings for children, after all, are what led you into coaching. Unfortunately, you must consider something else: Can you be held liable for the injury?

From a legal standpoint, a coach has nine duties to fulfill. We've discussed all but planning (see Unit 4) in this unit.

1. Provide a safe environment.
2. Properly plan the activity.
3. Make sure athletes have adequate and proper equipment.
4. Match skiers to appropriate terrain, skill, and competitive levels.
5. Warn of inherent risks in the sport.

6. Supervise the activity closely.
7. Evaluate athletes for injury or incapacity.
8. Know emergency procedures and first aid.
9. Keep adequate records.

In addition to fulfilling these nine legal duties, you should check your insurance coverage to make sure your present policy will protect you from liability.

Summary Self-Test

Now that you've read how to make your coaching experience safe for your skiers and you, test your knowledge of the material by answering these questions:

1. What are eight injury prevention measures you can institute to minimize the risk of injury to your skiers?
2. What method of treatment is best for minor sprains and strains?
3. What steps should you take to respond to serious injuries?
4. What weather conditions lead to cold emergencies, and what symptoms should you watch for?
5. What are the nine legal duties of a coach?

What Is Ski Racing All About?

ave you ever experienced the exhilaration of a ski race? You stand alone in the start, nervously waiting for the countdown that will signal you to begin. You push out of the start, pole hard to pick up some early speed, and begin gliding down through the gates. You feel cold wind on your face as you find the rhythm of the race course and let your skis run faster and faster. Crossing the finish line, your legs feel a little rubbery and you're breathing hard, but all you can think about was how good it felt to ski so fast!

Whether it's an 8-year-old in her first race or a 25-year-old in a championship event, the thrill is there for everyone. As a ski coach, you will have the fun of introducing kids to this exciting sport.

There is, though, a little more to it than setting up a course and letting your skiers go. The next three units of the *Rookie Coaches Ski Racing Guide* provide the ski racing basics you will need to do the job. Included are the basic rules, skills, tactics, and drills you and your ski racers should know.

Coaching Youth Ski Racing

Why take the time and trouble to coach ski racing? Perhaps the best reason is that kids love to race. Set a course, and they'll ski through the gates until the lifts close. Their enthusiasm makes them eager students, but part of the challenge of coaching is allowing kids to ski their fastest (and make mistakes) in an environment that is safe, not intimidating, and within their limits.

Ski racing is a little different from other youth sports. Although your kids don't have to be expert skiers, ski racing will be a safer, more positive experience for youngsters who are already comfortable on their skis and can make adequate parallel turns.

And your job as coach will also go more smoothly if you too can ski around the mountain with ease. Remember, the qualities that count the most to be a good ski coach are enthusiasm for kids and for ski racing and the ability to observe and teach.

What Are the Rules of Ski Racing?

Ski racing is a timed sport. Skiers race down through the gates of the course, trying to pass through them as fast as they can. Most races are two-run events. Racers take their first runs, then the course is reset and the racers take their second runs. Scoring is determined by combining each racer's first and second run times, then ranking those times in order. All competitors who successfully complete both runs figure into the race results.

Race courses are made up of a series of "gates" (a pair of poles set in the snow). The pole that the skiers are most likely to turn around is the "turning," or inside, pole. The other one is called the outside pole (see Figure 6.1 a and b). The turning pole is al-

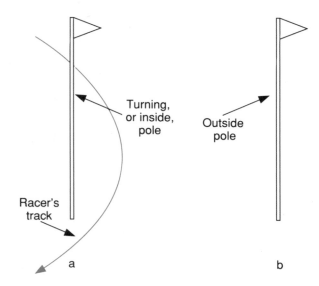

Figure 6.1 Slalom racers make turns through gates, made up of (a) "turning," or inside, poles and (b) outside poles.

ways a flex pole, which is hinged at its base and bends over when hit to make racing safer and less intimidating for skiers. (Don't be surprised to hear poles referred to as gates; the terms are often used interchangeably in ski racing.)

Slalom (see pages 37-38) poles have small flags tied on to the top. The gates for the other events are made up of pairs of poles attached by a cloth panel (see Figure 6.2). Two pairs of poles make up the turning pole and the outside pole for each gate. In all events except downhill, gates are set with alternat-

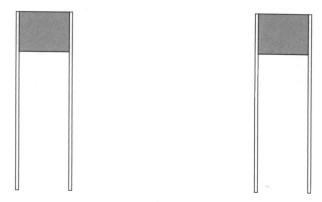

Figure 6.2 Pairs of poles attached by cloth panels are the outside and inside gates for giant slalom, super-g, and downhill.

ing red and blue poles (with matching flags or panels); in downhill all gates are red.

For a legal pass through each gate, a racer's skis and boots must cross the imaginary line connecting the poles (see Figure 6.3). Failure to pass through every gate results in disqualification (DSQ). Many fast ski racers knock the poles out of their way, but there is no penalty as long as both skis and boots have legally passed through each pair of poles. Likewise, racers are not penalized for falling down or taking gates in the wrong order or from the opposite direction than the other racers; it's just usually slower!

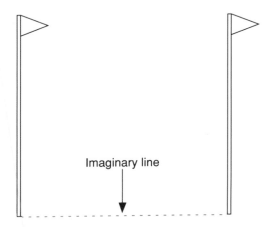

Figure 6.3 Racers' skis and boots must cross the imaginary line connecting the poles.

On race day, competitors are not allowed to practice on the race course before their runs (except for downhill). They are, however, given an inspection period to study the course with their coaches before they race. In addition, most coaches set a course on a nearby trail so skiers can practice and warm up before racing.

The Events

Alpine ski racing has four separate events: slalom, giant slalom, super-g, and downhill. Slalom and giant slalom are commonly referred to as the technical events, because they emphasize the technical skiing skills necessary to make good turns. Super-g and downhill are known as the speed events, although they require good technique, too! Table 6.1 lists the course specifications for these four events. Helmets are required for training and racing the speed events. Most young racers compete only in the technical events but train in speed elements to learn skills and gain experience so that they can eventually compete in speed events, too.

Slalom

Slalom (SL) is a test of agility and quickness because the slalom course has the most gates covering the shortest distance. Turns are quick and usually very rhythmical. Slalom is made up of several different types of gates—*open gates*, which are set laterally across the hill, and *closed gates*, which are set vertically down the hill and are used for setting special combinations like hairpins and flushes. *Hairpins* are made up of two closed gates in a row, and *flushes* have three or more closed gates in a row. Standard USSA-sanctioned slalom courses usually

Table 6.1
Course Specifications for USSA Races

	SL	GS	SG	DH
Minimum vertical drop (in meters)	120	250	350	400
Minimum # gates per run	42	30	30	
Approximate distance between turning poles (in meters)	8–12	12–20	15–30	
	.75–1 in slalom combinations			
Gate width (in meters)	4–6	4–8	8	8

Note. More information on course specifications is available by contacting the United States Ski Coaches Association. SL, slalom; GS, giant slalom; SG, super-g; DH, downhill. Vertical drop is the change in elevation from the start to the finish. Vertical drop measurements can be found on most trail maps that ski areas provide for their skiers.

include four hairpins and two flushes (see Figure 6.4).

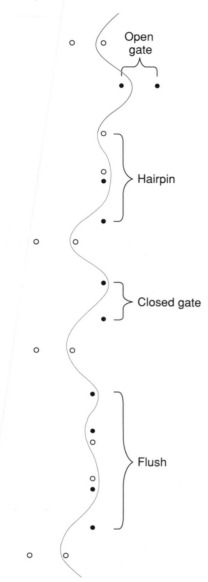

Figure 6.4 Gate combinations used in slalom courses.

Giant Slalom

Giant slalom (GS) is the event most like natural skiing, with bigger turns than in slalom. A well-set giant slalom course flows with the terrain and has a good rhythm. Coaches often start young or inexperienced racers on giant slalom, because it provides a good base from which to teach the other events. Most gates in giant slalom are open gates, although single closed gates may be used as well (see Figure 6.5).

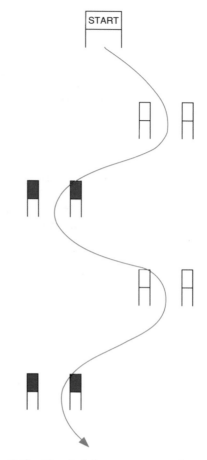

Figure 6.5 Giant slalom course with open gates.

Super-g

In super-g (SG), the turns are spread out further down the hill. Noted for its big turns and interesting use of terrain, super-g is a faster and longer race than giant slalom but speeds are still more controlled than downhill. Super-g is considered a speed event, so helmets are required and safety considerations are important.

Downhill

Downhill (DH) is the most exciting event, demanding courage and judgment as well as strength and technical skills. Downhill follows a trail down the mountain marked with a minimum number of gates to control speed and direct skiers.

Safety is very important in downhill. Officials make sure that the hill is well prepared and that fences and pads are placed to protect falling skiers from obstacles. At all levels, practice on the downhill course is mandatory before being allowed to race it.

Ski Racing Equipment

Ski racing requires a lot of equipment. Most of what you'll need for coaching should be supplied by your club, school, or ski area. Help keep costs reasonable for your racers by encouraging them to buy only what they really need and by organizing local ski swaps where your racers can buy and sell used equipment.

Racers' Equipment

The most essential equipment racers need are skis, boots, bindings, poles, eyewear and headgear, and warm clothes. Many ski racers have specialized gear that isn't really necessary for entry-level racers. Improvement in racing times for junior ski racers will come first by improving skills; only at advanced levels can equipment make a significant difference.

Skis

Skis have design features that help the skier turn. *Camber*, the bend or bow you see in the skis when you put them together, distributes the weight of the skier along the length of the ski. *Sidecut* is the difference in width between the middle (waist) of the ski and the tip and tail (see Figure 6.6). The more sidecut a ski has, the more it will turn. *Flex* is the spring resistance of the ski on the snow. Young, light skiers perform better on soft flexing skis, whereas heavier skiers require stiffer skis. Length affects the stability of the ski and the effort required to turn it. A longer ski is more stable at high speeds, whereas a short ski turns more easily.

Most junior skis have a good sidecut for quick turning, and a soft flex and relaxed camber so that kids can handle their skis comfortably. For the appropriate lengths for young kids, check Table 6.2.

Skis perform better when they are kept in good shape, with sharp edges and waxed bases. Occasionally invite a ski shop techni-

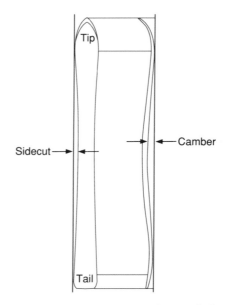

Figure 6.6 The camber and sidecut of skis make turning easier.

Table 6.2
Junior Ski Sizing Chart

Skier's weight	Ski size
30 lb	80 cm
40 lb	100 cm
50 lb	120 cm
60 lb	140 cm
70 lb	150 cm
80 lb	160 cm
90 lb	170 cm
100 lb	175 cm
110 lb	180 cm

cian to team meetings to help teach your skiers how to tune their skis.

Boots

Boots are designed to provide support, but they also must be flexible enough to allow the skier to bend the knee and ankle. Children usually need a softer boot than stronger, heavier adults. Most manufacturers have special junior racing models that are designed with the right combination of support and flex for young skiers. The skiers for whom boot selection is most critical are those teens whose feet have grown faster than the rest of them. It is important that the boots they wear not be too tall or too stiff. For all ski racers, a snug, comfortable fit is most important. Each brand of boots fits a little differently, so advise your skiers to get the boots that fit their feet the best and that flex well for them.

Bindings

Proper binding selection is essential for safe skiing. All binding manufacturers must meet stringent international standards. Specific models are designed for each skier's weight and ability level. Make sure that bindings are adjusted correctly and checked periodically by properly certified coaches or ski shop technicians.

Poles

Proper pole length is important for maintaining a quiet upper body and good balance (see Figure 6.7). To determine the proper length, turn the pole over so its tip is facing up. Have the skier grab the pole under the basket. If the poles are the correct length, the skier's forearm should be parallel to the ground.

Figure 6.7   How to determine proper pole length.

Eye and Head Protection

To protect their eyes from a collision with a gate, ski racers at every level must wear goggles, not sunglasses, when skiing courses. Make this mandatory for your program. When your skiers are free-skiing, encourage them to wear either sunglasses or goggles to protect their eyes from sun and wind damage.

Helmets are a must in downhill and super-g for both racing and training. Lightweight

head gear has been designed to protect faces from hitting gates when running slalom.

Clothing

Layered clothing will keep skiers warm and dry and allow them to adjust to changing conditions and work loads. Remind racers that their feet will stay warmer if they wear a clean pair of wool or wool blend socks each day. Many skiers wear padded racing sweaters, padded racing pants, and one-piece stretch suits, but such equipment certainly isn't necessary to get started in ski racing.

Encourage racers to bring a day pack with them to the ski area to carry extra clothes, sunscreen, a water bottle, and a snack or lunch. Remind your racers to use sunscreen and to drink water frequently. The sun is very strong in the mountains—sunburns and dehydration can occur even on cold days.

Equipment for Practices

Most of the equipment you'll need to gather for ski racing practices and competitions will be for setting courses and will be provided by your club, school, or ski area. Part of the coach's job is to order supplies and maintain team equipment in good working order.

Team Equipment

The poles you'll set your courses with are flex poles, or flex gates (see Figure 6.8). Made of plastic, they hinge near the bottom and will bend when hit. Bamboo poles are also commonly used and are much cheaper than flex gates. However, bamboo poles don't bend, which means skiers risk injury if they ski into the poles or break them. Many clubs use flex gates for turning poles and bamboo for the outside poles.

Use a cordless power drill, fitted with a long bit designed especially for course setting, to make holes in the snow for gate placement. Drill batteries wear down faster in cold conditions, so carry a couple of spare charged batteries.

Until racers are accustomed to them, sometimes the full-size gates can be more of a distraction than a help. See Figure 6.9 a-c for some teaching aids that can be useful:

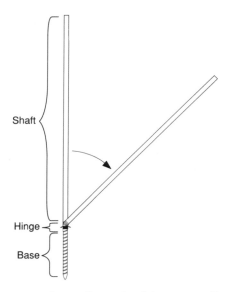

Figure 6.8 Plastic flex poles hinge near the bottom and bend when hit.

- Cones—the same small fluorescent cones used for soccer drills
- Stubby gates, or "stubbies"—flex gates with shafts about 2 ft long. Coaches create these out of broken full-size gates. Tape the tops of stubbies to eliminate sharp edges.
- Line markers—these are used to mark the line and must be small, unobtrusive, and safe to hit, but visible. Surveyor's flags work very well.

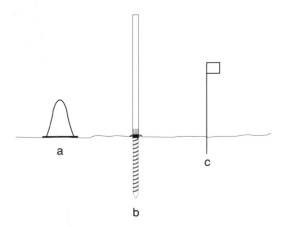

Figure 6.9 (a) Cones, (b) stubby gates, and (c) line markers will help learners adjust to full-size gates.

Coach's Equipment

If your club is well equipped, you may only have to worry about your own personal ski gear. A lot of coaching time is spent observing ski racers in action, which can mean standing around on cold days. Keep more warm clothes on hand than you think you'll need—you may end up wearing them. It is also a good idea to keep your own skis waxed and edges sharpened so that you'll ski your best when demonstrating and skiing with your racers.

Keep a stopwatch and a notepad and pencil in your parka pocket. A stopwatch can confirm for you what your eyes see and will come in handy for informal contests and timed training runs. When you are out on the hill with your skiers, you may think of ideas for another day's training, or you may make observations that you'd like to discuss with skiers later. Jotting them down in a notepad will help you remember later on.

Ski Racing Practices

Unlike soccer and baseball practices, where kids can meet a couple of evenings a week for an hour, ski racing practice is often more concentrated on the weekends, and sometimes after school. You may have your skiers for the full day, so you'll want to keep practice varied and fun and to build in breaks to keep your skiers fresh.

At most ski areas, you'll be able to ski with your skiers on any slope you wish as long as it is suited to their ability level and you are careful not to interfere with the skiing public. But when you want to give your skiers practice running gates, you will need to work closely with your ski area's staff, and you'll have to set courses.

Working With Ski Area Personnel

In some situations, coaches work directly for the ski area. Others work for clubs or schools that train at the area. Either way, advance planning with ski area personnel will make a big difference in how smoothly your practices go. Details to work out in advance include lift ticket costs, what time you can practice with your skiers, where you can set courses, and how often that slope will be groomed.

Many ski areas have one slope or trail that is set aside for race practice. You need to find out if it can be closed off for you and your skiers, if you will need to mark off a portion of the slope, or if you will have to set courses on the side of a trail open to the public. A closed trail is the safest but not always available. For variety, you may occasionally want to train on another part of the ski area. Ask well in advance and be cooperative, and you may be able to train where you'd like.

All ski areas have patrol personnel trained in first aid whose job is to come to the immediate aid of injured skiers. Area management will usually inform them about anything special going on, including your training. However, it is still a good idea to personally discuss your training schedule with them so that you all are prepared in case of an accident. At most areas, the ski patrol has good communication on the mountain and can get to an accident within a few minutes.

Finally, make sure your racers realize that you and your team need the ski area more than the other way around. Impress on your skiers the importance of making a positive impression by obeying all rules of the ski area and treating all personnel courteously.

Course Setting

Setting courses is one of the most creative aspects of coaching ski racing. It may also be a little intimidating if you have never done it before. But, just as racers have a progression to learn to run racecourses, you, too, will progress in learning to set courses. Here are some guidelines to help get you started:

Before Setting

- Be familiar with the hill. If the slope is new to you, ski it a couple of times before setting.
- Have a couple of people (other coaches or your racers) carry gates for you so you can concentrate on setting.
- Always keep the course away from trees, lift towers, and the edge of the trail. Safety is your top priority.
- Look ahead so you know where you are heading.
- Know the specifications for each event (see page 37). At first, distance is a little

hard to judge. Some coaches measure approximate distances with their skis (200 cm skis = 2 m) until they have gained enough experience to tell just by looking.

Getting Started

- When you are first learning to set courses, set only the turning poles, and focus on the rhythm and line you are setting for the racers. Have someone else set the outside poles or leave them out altogether until you start to get comfortable with setting. Practice courses are set both with and without outside poles, so it's okay to start with turning poles only.
- Start with short sections: 8 to 10 gates, on even-rhythm courses. Try to keep distances even. Set on smooth terrain.
- Gradually increase the number of gates that you set, and begin to experiment with varying the gate placement.

General Guidelines

- Make each course as rhythmical as you can. Simple back-and-forth gates are the easiest to set when first learning.
- Start each course with three to four open gates that establish a rhythm.
- Finish courses with three to four open gates that lead the skier directly to the middle of the finish.
- On the flats, set gates straighter down the hill so that racers can maintain some momentum.
- On the steeps, set gates across the hill to help racers control their speed.
- When approaching a steep section from the flats, begin slowing the racers down by gradually setting turns more across the hill before arriving at the steep pitch.

Special Consideration for Slalom Combinations

- When setting hairpins and flushes, consistency will make the timing easier for your skiers. Keep all gate distances the same. A recommendation is to make the gates 6 m long with .75 m between gates (see Figure 6.10).

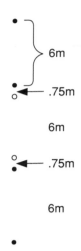

Figure 6.10 In slalom combinations, gates should be 6 meters long, with .75 meters between gates.

- Set gates so that the natural rhythm of the course will take the skier "over the top" of each vertical combination (see Figure 6.11 a and b). Setting this way is

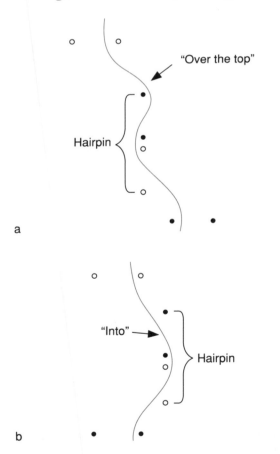

Figure 6.11 Gates set so the course will take skiers (a) "over the top" rather than (b) directly "into" the vertical combinations.

less confusing for the skier, more rhythmical, and controls the skier's speed better than sending the skier directly into the combinations.
- Set the combinations on the flats where the racers have less speed.

Additional Tips

- Always set "clean" courses—gates up straight, and gate widths consistent.
- Set the hinge of each gate exactly at the snow line. If the hinge is buried in the snow, the gate won't flex properly; if it's above the snow line, racers may ski into the unbending base of the pole.
- Learn from each course you set. Reset often. If the previous course seemed to make racers go too slowly, set the next course straighter or spread the gates down the hill a little more. If the previous course seemed to make skiers go excessively fast, set the gates on the next course either further across the hill, or shorten the vertical distance between gates so racers turn more.

What to Practice

Practicing gates is only one part of training for ski racing. To prepare skiers to race, your practices should cover three types of activities: technical skiing skills development, tactical gate training, and free-skiing. In any given practice, you may focus on one activity or a combination. For beginning racers, their time on snow in the course of a season should break down to approximately these percentages:

- 25% technical skiing skills development
- 25% tactical gate training
- 50% free-skiing

Developing the technical skiing skills of your ski racers is the focus of Unit 7. Unit 8 covers the tactics of ski racing. That leaves free-skiing, which is made up of directed skiing and ski play. Both methods are important and should be incorporated into your ski racers' time on the snow. Free-skiing doesn't have a whole unit to itself, but don't underestimate its importance in developing your ski racers' overall skiing ability.

Directed Skiing

Directed skiing is when you give your skiers something specific to work on while they are skiing. For example, you might say to one of your skiers, "Make every turn this afternoon on your outside ski." Ski with your racers during directed skiing. Many young racers learn best through imitation, so ski your best. You might have your racers follow in your tracks. Choose a variety of terrain and vary speed and turn size so that your skiers can practice their techniques in varied circumstances. Directed skiing reinforces skills learned through drills and helps form good habits.

Ski Play

Ski play emphasizes the mountain as a playground. By skiing with their buddies, your racers can expand their comfort zones by trying to keep up or by challenging others. They can explore varieties of terrain and conditions and discover the joy and freedom of skiing.

Ski Racing Terms to Know

Ski racing has its own vocabulary. Becoming familiar with common ski racing terms will make coaching easier.

across the fall line—Gates set across the fall line require the skis to complete the turn perpendicular to the fall line (or close to it).

angulation—The body's action to edge the ski and to balance on the edged ski.

carving—Cleanly edging the ski without skidding.

closed gate—A pair of poles between which the racer must pass, set vertically down the hill.

completion phase—The last part of the turn, where the skier must counteract the greatest force.

countering—The dynamic balancing of the upper body to the pressures built up in the turn by edging and pressure. In a countered position the shoulders are level and the upper body is directed downhill over the outside ski, aiming slightly toward the outside of the turn.

downhill ski—The ski that is down the hill from the other; in the turn, the ski that will be downhill at turn completion. Also called *outside ski*.

edge angle—The degree to which the ski is edged in the snow.

edging—The action of the skier placing the ski on edge to allow the skis to turn.

fall line—The line down a slope that gravity would follow. Picture it as the imaginary line a snowball would travel if rolling down the slope.

fall line turns—Turns requiring little direction change, where the skis mostly remain in the fall line.

flex pole—A pole that is hinged at the snow line so that it bends out of the way when hit by a racer. Also called *flex gate*.

fore–aft balance—Forward-and-back balance.

gate—Pairs of poles through which skis and boots must pass.

hip angulation—Edging the ski by moving the hips to the inside of a turn.

independent leg action—Moving easily from ski to ski.

initiation phase—The phase of the turn where the skis begin to be steered into the turn.

inside pole—The pole the racer turns around in each gate on a race course. Also called *turning pole*.

inside ski—The ski closest to the center of the turn.

knee angulation—Edging the ski by moving the knees in the direction the skier wants to turn.

lateral balance—Side-to-side balance.

line—The path a racer takes through the racecourse; where to ski in the course.

line markers—Small, unobtrusive, but visible flags used to point out the line.

open gate—A pair of poles between which the skier must pass, set horizontally across the hill.

outside pole—Used with the turning pole in

a gate to help mark the imaginary line the racer must cross.

outside ski—The ski farthest from the center of the turn, which controls the arc of the turn.

panel—The wide flag tied to two poles, pairs of which form gates for giant slalom, super-g, and downhill.

pole plant—The touch of a ski pole to the snow between turns; serves to signal the end of one turn and the beginning of the next.

preparation phase—The first phase of the turn, where the weight transfer takes place.

pressure control—Actively adjusting weight distribution for powerful turns.

rhythm—The tempo of turns, usually a repetitive beat.

rotary movement—Turning of the body to turn the skis in the same direction.

round turns—Turns requiring a great deal of direction change; round turn shape.

speed elements—The skills tested in the speed events.

steering—Guiding the skis into the turn by a twisting action of the lower legs in the direction of the turn. Used with edging in advanced levels.

stubby gates—Flex gates with 2 ft shafts used to introduce slalom; also called *stubbies*.

tactics—The strategy of where and when to turn in a race course.

technique—Basic skiing skills.

timing—When to turn in a race course to maintain momentum while racing.

traverse—Skiing straight across the hill from one side of a slope to the other.

tuck—A low, aerodynamic position on skis.

turning phase—The middle portion of the turn where the most direction change occurs; edging and pressure increase greatly during this phase.

turning pole—See *inside pole*.

uphill ski—Ski that is uphill of the other. Also called *inside ski*.

vertical combinations—Hairpins and flushes in a slalom course.

vertical drop—The change in elevation from one point to another (usually start to finish).

weight distribution—Where the skier's weight falls on the skis.

weight transfer—Shifting the skier's weight from one ski to the other.

What Skiing Skills and Drills Should I Teach?

efore the kids on your team can become good ski racers, they must first become good skiers. As their skiing skills improve, your racers will be able to make quicker turns, ski faster lines through race courses, handle steeper terrain, and race with more confidence. This unit focuses on how to teach skills necessary for ski racing. Unit 8 will show you how to help your racers apply these skills on race courses.

What Basic Skiing Skills Are Important?

You may wonder what skills to emphasize to your racers. It probably seems like there's so much to teach, it's hard to know where to begin! A good place to start is with the four basic skills involved in the parallel turn. In this unit, you'll learn how to teach these skills, along with drills to teach and reinforce them. Then we'll put them all together to develop and link parallel turns and apply parallel turns to a variety of skiing situations.

These are the four basic technical skills found in every good parallel turn:

- *Balancing*
- *Rotary movements*
- *Edging*
- *Pressure control*

Balancing

Because of the changing conditions on a ski slope, good balance is a dynamic, ongoing challenge for all skiers. If a racer is struggling to maintain balance, it is hard to focus on the techniques and tactics required to be fast.

There are two kinds of balancing to focus on for skiing: fore–aft balancing and lateral balancing. In addition, the upper body plays a significant role.

Fore–Aft Balancing

Fore–aft, or forward-and-back, balancing is the ability to keep weight under the foot, not too far forward on the ski tips or too far back on the tails of the skis. As a skier accelerates out of a turn, or as the skis gain momentum down the hill faster than the skier, the skier's weight tends to fall back over the tails. This is especially true with junior racers.

To keep ski racers centered over their skis, teach them to stay forward. Skiers balance by flexing the ankles and feeling the pressure of the tongue of the ski boot on the shin, while keeping the hips over the boots and arms forward (see Figure 7.1).

Some kids ski stiff-legged. Reminding them to bend their knees may be all you need to do. If their hips fall back when they bend their knees, it may be that their boots are too stiff. If so, loosen the top buckle so that their ankles flex when their knees bend.

Figure 7.1   Fore-aft balancing is keeping weight centered over the feet.

Lateral Balancing

Lateral, or side-to-side, balancing is essential throughout the turn. The best stance for good lateral balancing is having the feet hip-width apart. Have your skiers balance on one ski and then move easily from ski to ski to help them develop good lateral balance. A very wide stance may seem more stable, but it makes it difficult to move from ski to ski.

The Upper Body's Role

A steady, calm upper body allows the skier to focus attention on the lower body, where the real action is taking place. A "quiet" upper body, with the shoulders level, helps maintain lateral balance. The arms are more important for balancing the body than you might think, especially in fore–aft balance. Teach skiers to carry their arms about chest height and in front, within view of their peripheral vision. Except for regaining balance, there shouldn't be excessive arm movements.

Balanced Stance

Just like other sports, skiing starts with an athletic, relaxed, "ready" stance. However, balancing for skiing is balancing in motion—dynamic balancing. Having the greatest possible range of motion around the ideal balanced stance helps skiers increase their agility in handling a variety of turns in changing terrain. The basic stance in skiing includes these elements (see Figure 7.2):

- All joints slightly flexed
- Feet hip-width apart
- Weight centered evenly between and along both feet
- Hips over feet, with the back slightly rounded
- Hands out front and raised to within the skier's view
- Shoulders level
- Head up and eyes looking ahead

Figure 7.2   A balanced stance in motion.

Balance in motion helps skiers react to the unexpected, recover faster, and recenter their weight quickly. Balancing is such an important skill that you should incorporate some formal balance work into every single practice session.

Balancing Drills

Name. **Straight Running**

Purpose. To help racers get a feel for a balanced stance.

Organization. Find a gentle slope where skiers can go straight downhill without gaining much speed. Have skiers assume a balanced stance and run their skis straight down the hill for about 20 meters. Demonstrate first. Start above your skiers so they can see views from below, beside, and above. Have them go

one at a time and stop after they have passed you. Repeat the drill.

Coaching Point. Make sure skiers have skis hip-width apart, ankles flexed, knees bent, hips over boots, and arms out front. They should be relaxed, not holding a stiff pose, and looking ahead. With each skier, focus on one aspect to correct.

Variation. In a straight run, have skiers alternate lifting the ski tips one at a time off the snow; then repeat the drill with skiers lifting the tails. This will improve their fore–aft balancing. In a straight run, have skiers "walk" down the hill, alternately lifting one whole ski, then the other, about 2 inches off the snow. This will help their lateral balancing.

Name. **Ski Pole Drill**

Purpose. To work on a quiet upper body facing downhill, with level shoulders and arms forward.

Organization. Choose an intermediate slope. Have skiers take off their ski poles, put them together grip-to-basket, and hold them as if they were holding a tray. Skiers imagine their trays hold mugs of hot chocolate, and they must make turns all the way to the bottom without spilling a drop.

Coaching Point. If you demonstrate first, you can ski down and watch from below. You want to see skiers' poles staying level and quiet in front of them (see Figure 7.3). If you

Figure 7.3   Skiers' poles should be level, steady, and in front on the turns.

see poles tipping inside on each turn, the shoulders aren't staying level because the skier is leaning in. Correct this by instructing the skier to tip the tray to the outside on each turn.

Figure 7.4 For the skiing on one ski drill, beginners can wear both skis and just lift one.

SKI TIP

For all drills, remember to choose terrain that is not intimidating for your skiers, so they can concentrate on the skill they are trying to master.

Name. **Skiing on One Ski**

Purpose. To improve balance and coordination.

Organization. Select an easy slope. Beginning racers can lift one ski a few inches off the snow and try to make a series of turns on the other ski. More advanced racers can remove one ski and ski down the hill with only the other ski (first get permission for your skiers to ride the lift, or have them partner up and take turns carrying each others' skis). Ask your skiers to make short turns (see Figure 7.4).

Coaching Point. At first this drill may be hard for your skiers. Be encouraging and make it fun. Skiing on one ski takes a lot of strength, so only ask your skiers to try it a little bit at any one time. Gradually their bodies will adapt to the narrower balance point, and

they will get the hang of it. This drill improves balance and agility enormously without any technical talk from the coach.

Rotary Movement

Rotary movement is a steering action that helps guide the skis into the fall line and engage the edges smoothly. In ski racing, rotary movements are done in coordination with edging movements.

Steering is done with the lower body. When skiing at slow speeds, your skiers can simply turn their feet and point them in a desired direction. The skis will follow in the direction

---

Error Detection and Correction for Balancing

A common problem for young skiers is keeping their weight forward.

ERROR	CORRECTION
The racer's hips fall back behind his or her boots, which compromises control.	1. Have the skier bend knees forward and feel the shins pressing against the tongue of the boot and feel their weight on the toes and ball of the foot.
	2. Make sure the skier can flex the boots. Loosen the top boot buckle if necessary.
	3. Move the arms up and forward.

of the toes. As turn size and speed increases, it is necessary to involve the lower legs and knees in the guiding process, by aiming with the knees (see Figure 7.5).

Figure 7.5 The lower legs and knees are used in steering.

Have your skiers concentrate on steering into their turns with their weight predominantly on the outside leg. Their inside leg should help to guide the skis through the turn. As skiers guide the inside ski parallel to, and slightly ahead of, the outside ski, they can execute turns quickly and accurately.

If a skier doesn't actively guide the skis with the legs, the rotary movement will still occur but not as efficiently. The alternative to guiding with the legs is to twist the upper body in the direction the skier wishes to turn. The direction change will be made, but the tails of the skis will skid, slowing the skier down. Using the legs gives the skier more control and speed.

Rotary Movement Drills

Name. **Headlights**

Purpose. To introduce guiding of the skis by steering with the legs.

Organization. Start on a gentle slope. Skis should be in a slight wedge position to control speed. Ask your skiers to think of themselves as cars; their knees become head-

lights. Have them ski down, letting their headlights point the way. Next, move to an intermediate slope and repeat at more moderate speeds.

Coaching Point. This skill comes easily to most skiers. This drill teaches your skiers awareness of rotary movement and can help those who struggle a little with starting new turns.

Name. **Hockey Stops**

Purpose. To emphasize the lower body's role in rotary movement.

Organization. Choose a smooth intermediate-level slope. Start your skier with a balanced stance in a straight run. Once the skier builds up speed (within 10 meters or so), the skier should pivot the feet quickly underneath the body until the skis point across the hill. Edge abruptly to stop. Start skiers one at a time. Repeat several times to each side (see Figure 7.6).

Coaching Point. When properly done, the upper body will stay facing downhill and the tracks will have stayed in the fall line. It sometimes takes young skiers a while to separate their quiet upper bodies from their more active lower bodies. If they lose balance as they pivot their skis and stop, they should work on keeping their balance forward.

Figure 7.6 The abrupt pivot to a stop in the hockey stop drill.

Name. **Finding the Fall Line**

Purpose. To highlight guiding the skis into the turn.

Organization. Find a wide easy to intermediate slope that is free of other skiers. Have your skiers start from a traverse with their skis headed across the hill. As they push off, they should flatten their skis and steer with their feet and knees until their skis find the fall line; then they should stop with a hockey stop. The inside ski should lead the outside ski by an inch or two. Have your skiers repeat these half turns several times in each direction.

Coaching Point. This drill is good for the awareness of the natural role that steering plays in getting into each turn. Make sure your racers relax and don't try to force the ski. Point out to your skiers that gravity helps make finding the fall line easier. When properly done, the racers' skis will leave smooth clean tracks in the snow.

Edging

Edging provides the control necessary to turn cleanly. Without good edging skills, your skiers will not have the control to turn quickly and powerfully at any speed.

To edge a ski, the skier rolls the ski up on its edge (see Figure 7.7). If pressure is then applied to the edged ski, the ski will turn and carve an arc in the snow. This allows a skier to turn precisely and efficiently. The imprint left in the snow will show clean tracks. There are a couple of ways to roll the skis up on edge. One method is to lean the whole body in, but this can throw the skier out of balance and slow her down. A better way is to either

Figure 7.7   Edging a ski means rolling the ski up on its edge.

roll the knees to one side (knee angulation) or move the hip to the inside (hip angulation). Whatever the type of angulation, rolling a tracking ski up on edge is more precise and controlled than pushing the ski out on edge.

Hip Angulation

With hip angulation the skis and feet are well to the outside of the body. The farther out the skis are away from the body, the more edge angle the skier will have (see Figure 7.8).

Knee and Ankle Angulation

Instruct your skiers to use knee and ankle angulation when they need to make quick, short turns in the fall line and to fine-tune the edge angle in rounder turns. When knee and ankle angulation is applied, the skis stay under the body (see Figure 7.9).

Error Detection and Correction for Rotary Movement

If skiers don't actively steer the skis with their legs, they must force the skis around by twisting the upper body in the direction they want to turn instead.

ERROR	CORRECTION
The skier uses upper body rotation to turn, which causes the tails of the skis to slide out and the skier to lose control.	1. Review steering with the legs, especially at the beginning of the turn. 2. Repeat rotary movement drills. 3. Repeat "Ski Pole Drill" from the balance section.

Figure 7.8 With hip angulation, the skis and feet move out from under the body while the upper body counters the activity of the lower body.

Figure 7.9 With knee and ankle angulation, the skis stay under the body.

Edging and the Upper Body

The upper body counterbalances the activity taking place in the lower body. The natural tendency for many young ski racers is to lean in, which causes the skis to slide out of control. To counter this tendency, teach skiers to keep their shoulders level and to lead slightly with the inside hand and shoulder. This will turn the upper body toward the outside of the turn, and the skier will bend forward slightly (see Figure 7.8). This countering allows racers to edge more precisely and ski more powerfully.

How Much Edge Is Needed?

Racers need a greater edge angle when the hill is steep, the turn is sharp, or the snow is hard. If the slope is flat, the turn is a gradual one, or conditions are soft, your racers should minimize edge angles. Practice will improve your skiers' feel for the right amount of edge needed in a given situation. The skis must be edged enough to turn cleanly and precisely; however, excessively digging the edges into the snow will slow the racer down.

The amount of edge angle needed also varies within each turn. At the beginning of a turn, gravity helps the skier find the fall line with a minimum amount of edging. The opposite is true at the end of a turn. When the skis leave the fall line, gravity and other

---

Error Detection and Correction for Edging

Sometimes young skiers push their skis out to create an edge, instead of cleanly rolling the ski up on edge. This causes the skis to slide until the edge is engaged.

ERROR	**CORRECTION**
The skier pushes the ski to edge it, resulting in a skidding ski and loss of control.	1. Make sure the skier's edges are sharp.
	2. Standing still, demonstrate the difference between pushing the ski out, and rolling it up on edge. Have skiers practice until they can feel the difference.
	3. On an easy slope, have skiers roll the knees from side to side to feel the correct way to engage the edges.

forces work against the skier. Progressively increasing the edge angle throughout the turn will allow the skier to finish the turn cleanly and powerfully.

Edging Drills

Name. **Traverse**

Purpose. To introduce edging.

Organization. Choose a wide slope free of public skiers. Start at one side of the slope. Have your skiers point their skis at a point across the hill that is slightly lower than where they are standing. One at a time, skiers push off, roll the skis up on edge, and ride the edged ski across the hill (see Figure 7.10). Repeat in each direction. Alternate between releasing the edges by flattening the skis against the snow (sideslipping) and edging.

Coaching Point. Show your skiers when they sideslip that their tracks are skidded, but when they edge their skis, their tracks are clean. Make sure they notice that sideslipping feels sloppy, while edging gives them more control.

Figure 7.10 The body position for the traverse drill.

Name. **Red Light, Green Light**

Purpose. To improve edge control.

Organization. On a steep but smooth slope, spread skiers out with their skis edged and pointing across the hill. Stand below them. On your signal (either a verbal "green light"

or a wave of your poles), the skiers release their edges and begin sideslipping down the hill. When you signal "red light," they must stop immediately. To stop, they'll need to edge hard. Repeat several times with skiers facing each direction.

Coaching Point. This is a fun game that teaches good control of the edges. This drill works best on hard snow. Skiers will totally stop if the snow's too soft.

Name. **Carving Drill**

Purpose. To feel how the edges help the ski turn.

Organization. Choose a wide, gentle intermediate slope free of skier traffic. Start your skiers in a balanced position with their skis pointed downhill. Have your skiers push off and immediately roll their skis on the left edge. They should just stand on the edged skis, which will carve an arc through the snow ending in a traverse to the left. Repeat to both sides.

Coaching Point. Check your skiers' tracks. Clean tracks show that the skiers let the edges carve. If the racers force their skis around, tracks will be skidded. Because your skiers are only edging and not steering, the arcs their skis make will be gradual, but that's okay. This drill will give your skiers a nice feel for how their edges work.

Pressure Control

Skis are your racers' tools. Applying pressure to the ski bends it like a bow and, when combined with edging, results in turning. Controlling pressure includes making active adjustments such as weight distribution, flexion/extension movements, and edging.

Weighting the Outside Ski

A key skill for making racing turns is putting weight on the outside ski. By concentrating all of the pressure (weight) on one ski, it will react more forcefully. This allows the skier to make cleaner, quicker, more powerful turns than if the skier's weight is evenly distributed between both skis. Teach your skiers the feeling of weighting the outside ski by having them shift their weight from ski to ski on a series of easy turns. Have them weight the outside ski, then quickly shift weight to the other ski to begin the next turn (see Figure 7.11 a and b). Even though both skis are steered and edged, only the outside ski is weighted in most turns.

Figure 7.11 Shifting weight from (a) one outside ski to (b) the other will allow the skier to make more powerful turns.

Independent leg action allows the skier to shift weight from one outside ski to the other. This is a vital skill in the race against the clock. If the hill is steep, the turn is tight, or the conditions are icy, 100% of the skier's weight should be on the outside ski. If the slope is flat, the turn shallow, or the conditions soft, a ski racer should still have 70% of the weight on the outside ski. The inside ski rests lightly on the snow, actively steering, edging, and balancing. Have your racers focus on the difference in feeling both 100% and 70% of their weight on the outside ski during runs on various terrain.

Fore–Aft Weight Distribution

In each turn, pressure moves along the ski from tip to tail. This pressure is controlled under the skier's foot. At the beginning of the turn, the skier's weight is forward, under the ball of the foot, and the skier presses the shins against the tongue of the boots. This transfers pressure to the front of the ski, and it begins to turn. Through the turn, the skier's weight moves from the ball of the foot to the heel. It is unnecessary and incorrect to lean far forward or back to pressure the skis; the control is all under the foot.

The problem for most junior skiers is when the momentum of the turn forces their weight back on to the tails. Once "in the back seat" many youngsters lack the strength to pull themselves forward again. Not only is this inefficient, but also knee injuries may occur because of the strain on the ligaments. Therefore, most juniors need to concentrate on staying forward to maintain balance. Skiers should adopt a centered stance of the hips over the boots, shoulders rounded, and arms out front. The key is to be forward for the beginning of each turn.

Using the Edges

As the forces build throughout the turn, an increasing edge angle helps to resist those forces and keep the skis turning cleanly. Pressure on the ski increases throughout the turn as the edge angle increases. Turns made in this manner are quite powerful.

Up and Down Motion

In between the turns, skiers transfer their weight from the "old" outside ski to the "new" outside ski. For young kids to do this, there can't be much pressure on the skis. During the turn, though, a lot of pressure builds up on the skis and the skier's hips are in a relatively low position because of angulation. One way to reduce the pressure in between the turns is to raise the hips at the end of the turn as the skis flatten out. This puts the skier in a taller, more relaxed stance and makes the weight transfer an easier one. Raising the hips should be a gradual motion to maintain the flow of turning. The "taller" stance in between turns is not a straight-legged one; teach your skiers to keep knees bent enough to absorb any bumps or terrain changes.

Pressure Control Drills

Name. **Outside Ski Turns**

Purpose. To practice transferring pressure from outside ski to outside ski.

Organization. On an intermediate slope, have your skiers make a series of turns, lifting the inside ski in each turn (see Figure 7.11 a and b). This guarantees that 100% of the weight is on the outside ski.

Coaching Point. Normally, skiers keep the inside ski on the snow for balance, but this drill lets you see if your skiers can keep all of their weight on the outside ski. This also helps their balance. Your skiers are most likely to run into a problem at the end of the turn when the forces have built up. A good countered upper body (level shoulders, inside shoulder ahead, arms driving forward, upper body leaning forward and tipped slightly toward the outside) will solve this.

Name. **Falling Leaf**

Purpose. To show how controlling the pressure under the foot affects the ski.

Organization. On a steep smooth slope, have skiers sideslip slowly down the hill. While they are side slipping, have them move their weight to the ball of the foot; the skis will slide forward. Then have them shift their weight back to their heels, and the skis will slide back. Repeat each direction; their skis make a pattern like a leaf slowly falling through the air.

Coaching Point. The skiers' movements should be subtle, with the action taking place under the foot. For beginning racers, this is easier to do with a little speed and on hard snow.

Name. **Leaper**

Purpose. To practice an up-and-down motion.

Organization. Use a smooth intermediate slope. Have skiers make some turns at moderate speeds. In between turns, have skiers leap up until their skis come off the snow a little, then land and turn, leaping and turning down the hill.

Error Detection and Correction for Pressure Control

In the excitement of racing, sometimes ski racers end up with their weight distributed on both skis or even on the inside ski, causing the outside ski to slide out.

ERROR	CORRECTION
The skier leans in, shifting the weight off the outside ski.	1. Have the skier skate across the flats to get the feel of going from ski to ski.
	2. On easy terrain, have your skier make small turns from outside ski to outside ski, touching the outside knee with the outside hand on each turn (see Figure 7.12).
	3. Remind the skier about countering: keeping the shoulders level, slightly tipped to the outside, with the inside arm leading and outside arm reaching over the outside ski.

Figure 7.12 As practice, a skier touches the outside knee with the outside hand on turns.

Coaching Point. This drill exaggerates the motion your skiers should make, but it gives them a good feel for what they are trying to do. A lot of young skiers hold a static position on their skis. Leaping between turns gets skiers' legs up between the turns and down in the turns.

Parallel Turns

Now your skiers have all the basic skills. The next step is to put it all together in the parallel turn. How does the ski racer combine the skills of balance, rotary movements, edging, and pressure control into well-executed parallel turns? Let's examine the phases of the parallel turn to see how the components fit together.

In every turn, two main forces affect the skier. Gravity is constantly pulling the skier down the hill while centrifugal force pulls the skier out of the turn. In the early phases of the turn, gravity and centrifugal force counterbalance each other. However, in the second half of the turn, they combine forces against the skier (see Figure 7.13).

The four phases of the turn that you need to teach are preparation, initiation, turning, and completion (see Figure 7.14).

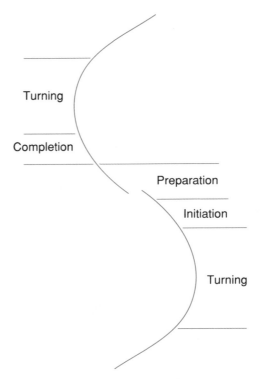

Figure 7.14 The four phases of turning: preparation, initiation, turning, and completion.

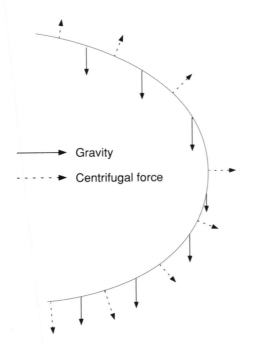

Figure 7.13 The pulls of gravity and centrifugal force during a parallel turn.

Preparation Phase

In the preparation phase, your skiers are getting ready to begin a turn. They must shift their weight from the old outside ski to the new outside ski. A pole plant (see p. 59) can help a skier initiate this weight shift. Teach your skiers to make sure they are balanced and centered on their skis before proceeding with the turn (see Figure 7.15a).

Initiation Phase

In the initiation phase, your skiers will steer their skis with light edging into the turn. They should shift their weight forward, raising their hips and projecting their hips and upper bodies down the hill (see Figure 7.15b). This phase is crucial in racing, because skiers make their commitment to choosing the right line in the initiation phase.

Turning Phase

In the turning phase, your skiers are traveling into, down, and out of the fall line. Both pressure and edging are essential components of turning. Remind your skiers to

Figure 7.15 The four phases of a parallel turn: (a) preparation, (b) initiation, (c) turning, and (d) completion.

concentrate on pressure and edging to control their speed most effectively when turning. Show them how to lead slightly with their inside arm, hip, and ski as they move through each turn to put themselves in a good countered position (see Figure 7.15c).

Completion Phase

The strongest forces during a turn are exerted against the skier as he or she turns out of the fall line. A countered position of level shoulders, inside arm leading, and both arms forward is necessary to maintain good balance during the completion phase (see Figure 7.15d). By maintaining this countered position throughout the turn, the end of the completion phase should blend smoothly into the preparation phase for the next turn.

Parallel Turn Drill

Name. **Parallel Turn**

Purpose. To put balance, rotary movements, edging, and pressure control together into the parallel turn.

Organization. Choose an intermediate slope. Have your skiers make one turn, stop, and repeat in the other direction. Have them start in a traverse, push off, and steer their skis toward the fall line with the skis lightly edged. As they approach the fall line, they increase the edge angle. At this point, the pressure is beginning to build up in the turn. As they increase the edge, they push down on the big toe of the outside ski. The pressure and edge angle builds until the turn is complete and the skis are in a traverse again.

Coaching Point. Keep this simple for your skiers. Stress the feel of developing edge and pressure throughout the turn. As they finish each turn with a traverse, check to see if they are balanced and ready for the next turn.

Pole Plants

The pole plant is used to trigger the end of one turn and the beginning of the next. The downhill pole is extended to plant as the previous turn ends and the skier is extending. Skiers in balance at the completion of a turn prepare for the pole plant by cocking the wrist back so that the pole swings forward. They then lightly tap the pole in the snow, triggering the weight transfer (see Figure 7.16). In steep terrain, skiers use a more aggressive pole plant as they reach down the hill to plant the pole more firmly. In either case, skiers need to keep arm movement fluid and precise. The pole should touch down ahead of the skier in the direction of travel.

Figure 7.16 The pole plant marks the end of one turn and the beginning of the next and helps the skier maintain balance.

Skiers should then transfer their weight and begin the next turn.

Besides a timing device, planting the pole also helps skiers maintain balance. Have your skiers keep their hands in front of their bodies and plant their pole slightly downhill. This pole plant will help the skier project the hips and upper body forward and down the hill. It also helps skiers reestablish or maintain a balanced position between turns.

Pole Plant Drill

Name. **Pole Plant Timing**

Purpose. To practice the timing of pole plants.

Organization. On a gentle slope, start skiers from a traverse. The focus will be on the pole plant and not the turn itself. Have them extend the legs, plant the downhill pole, slide the skis around to a new traverse, then extend the legs, plant the pole, slide around, and continue down the hill. As they establish a rhythm, skiers can clean up their turns and add a little speed.

Coaching Point. Have your skiers follow you closely down the hill, imitating your timing. You can also establish a rhythm with your voice, giving a "hup" whenever it is time to plant.

Linking Parallel Turns

Ski racers must be able to link turns on race courses made up of 40 or more turns. Linking parallel turns is a matter of "staying with" each turn throughout its completion and then smoothly making the transition to the next turn.

Junior ski racers often start out with a few good turns, gradually pick up speed, and make larger and larger turns that are more and more in the fall line. By the bottom of the run, they are skiing very fast, but with very little control. Part of the problem is that they are not completing their turns. Remind your skiers to "stay with" and complete each turn to maintain the control necessary for a good, clean, fast run. Discipline your racers to concentrate on turn completion in each run no matter what the terrain.

Drills for Linking Parallel Turns

Name. **Follow the Leader**

Purpose. To practice linking complete turns.

Organization. Have skiers follow you or another good skier who can link consistent turns down the hill rhythmically. The followers must stay exactly in the tracks of the leader. A variation is to pair skiers, giving each one the chance to be the leader. When they lead, they must set the example of good turns.

Coaching Point. Follow the leader works especially well for skiers who learn by imitating. Linking turns isn't usually a matter of technique as much as it is discipline, so the controlled environment this drill provides—for both follower and leader—is usually enough.

Name. **Turn Contest**

Purpose. To practice linking complete turns.

Organization. Choose a moderate to steep slope. See who can make the most turns in 50 meters. Winner gets a hot chocolate!

Coaching Point. This contest, like the preceding drill, is fun. Your skiers will be practicing and reinforcing good skills without even realizing it.

Versatility

As you work with your ski racers, their ability to make and link parallel turns will improve.

So far, the focus has been on the drills, with terrain chosen specifically to allow your skiers to concentrate on learning skills with few variables. The next step for your racers is to try parallel turns in more challenging conditions.

Vary where your racers ski and train. Start easy, but once your skiers have mastered gentle terrain, move to a more challenging slope. Allow your skiers to build confidence as they gain experience. Ski moguls, steeps, flats; even the easiest trails are great for gliding and developing a light touch. Encourage your skiers to experiment with a variety of turn sizes and shapes. Ultimately, you want your skiers to automatically apply the skills you have taught them without even thinking about it. If a ski racer's career is shaped like a pyramid, the eventual success of the skier, or height of the pyramid, will be determined by the breadth of the base. Establish a strong fundamental base for your skiers. Versatility is the key!

Skiing terrain that is too challenging all the time will not help young skiers progress. If conditions seem too difficult, young skiers will start braking and making technical errors. Begin with easy skiing to build confidence and skills, then challenge them with steeper slopes. Always follow challenging runs with some easier ones to reinforce the good parallel turns you've helped them acquire.

UNIT 8

What Racing Tactics Should I Teach?

rriving at the top of a racecourse can be an intimidating experience for first-time ski racers. As they look down the race hill, it may look like a confusion of red and blue gates.

Ski racing doesn't have to be that way for your racers. The sport is fun, and their introduction to ski racing should be fun, too. If their first experience in the gates is easy and successful, they will be eager to head back up and try it again. Introducing your skiers to racing in a gradual, systematic way will build their confidence. And, more importantly, they'll enjoy their ski racing experience every step of the way, including the first one!

This unit shows you how to introduce ski racing to your skiers in a safe, nonthreatening way. You'll learn what racing tactics to teach and what specific situations your racers are likely to encounter. Guidelines for teaching racing tactics are outlined, including sample progressions for developing slalom and giant slalom experiences. The unit ends with some considerations of race day, when your racers put their skills to the test.

Introducing Skiers to Race Courses

Young kids can discover the fun of skiing gates even if they are not ready to learn about racing tactics. A great way to introduce ski racing is to head to an easy slope and set a course made of small fluorescent cones like you would use for soccer drills. Place six to eight cones down the hill at about 10-meter intervals. Offset them just enough so that your skiers have to turn as they pass by each cone.

From the top of the course, point out the cones and lead your skiers down through them. If they follow right behind you, they will have a feel for the course and a good track will be set. Have them follow the tracks a few times on their own.

Incorporate these cone courses into practice sessions that are primarily focused on skiing skills development. Repeat these courses a few times, and your skiers will begin to be comfortable with turning around objects in the snow.

The next step is setting gates. At this stage don't worry about outside poles; set only the turning (inside) pole. If you alternate red and blue poles down the hill, tell your skiers to look for the next blue pole as they ski around a red pole, and vice versa. Continue to set the track for them to follow; but instead of giving instructions to follow the tracks, tell them on which side of the gate to ski.

During this introductory stage, don't correct any technical errors you see—just provide encouragement. As your skiers improve, they'll become more comfortable skiing gates. Then you can introduce racing tactics.

Basic Elements of Ski Racing

You might think that ski racing is just turning at each gate, but racers have momentum and gravity to contend with. Line (where to ski) and timing (when to turn) are two elements the ski racer needs to master to maintain speed all the way through a racecourse.

Line

Line is the path the racer takes through the gates. A good line takes the skier smoothly and speedily from one section of the course to the next. The best line at any gate allows the racer to complete the turn cleanly and be on track for the next gate. This line is determined by where the next two gates are placed. Teaching line is teaching your ski racers where to aim. Junior skiers will be tempted to aim directly at the gate. But if they do so, they will have no room to turn. Instead, instruct your skiers to aim at the place in the snow above the gate where they plan to start their turn.

Gates Set Across the Fall Line

Gates set across the fall line mean that each turn has a big change of direction (see Figure 8.1). These turns take more space to negotiate smoothly. Therefore, as the racer finishes

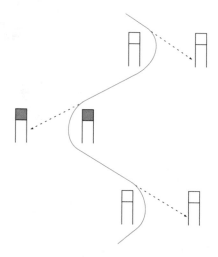

Figure 8.1 Gates set across the fall line require a big change of direction at each turn. Aiming toward the outside pole of the upcoming gate helps the racer line up correctly for the turn.

one turn and heads toward the next, the racer must set up for the next turn by aiming for the outside pole of the upcoming gate. This puts the racer well above the gate at the rise line, which is an imaginary line running up the hill from the turning pole, and allows room for the racer to finish a clean turn with the skis aiming at the next outside pole. This line is often referred to as a *round line*.

Gates Set in the Fall Line

When the gates are set for a more direct run down the hill, the racer can aim more toward the inside of the gate (still not directly at the inside pole: see Figure 8.2). This is a straighter, more direct line. Inexperienced racers get themselves into trouble when they try to apply this straighter line in round turns. Conversely, a round line in a straight section of turns will be slow.

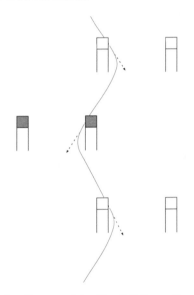

Figure 8.2   Gates set in the fall line allow for a more direct run down the hill.

Timing

The initiation phase occurs at the midpoint between gates. The turning phase begins as the racer crosses the rise line (see Figure 8.3). Waiting for the rise line can be hard for impatient junior racers, who are tempted to rush into the turn, crowd the gate, and are then forced to turn below the gate. Teach your ski racers the more patient approach of waiting for the rise line so that they can begin

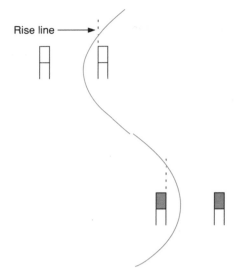

Figure 8.3   The rise line is an imaginary line running up the hill from the turning pole.

to complete the turn as they brush past the gate, already aiming in the new direction (see Figures 8.1 and 8.2).

Timing and Line Drill

Name. **Timing and Line**

Purpose. To introduce timing and line.

Organization. Choose a smooth slope with a gentle to moderate pitch. Set 8 to 10 even-rhythm gates back and forth down the fall line. Use a line marker to mark the intersection above each gate of the rise line and the line aiming toward the outside gate (see Figure 8.4). Either reset often (every four

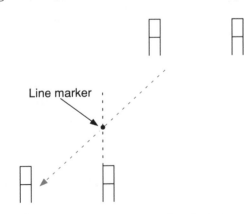

Figure 8.4   A line marker marks the intersection of the rise line with the line aiming toward the outside gate.

Error Detection and Correction for Timing and Line

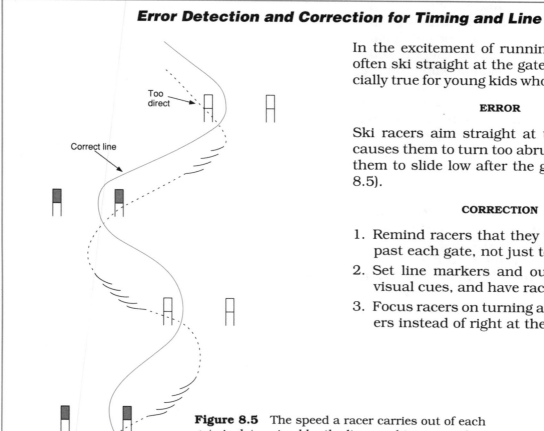

Figure 8.5 The speed a racer carries out of each gate is determined by the line used to approach the gate.

In the excitement of running gates, skiers often ski straight at the gates. This is especially true for young kids who like to ski fast.

ERROR

Ski racers aim straight at the gates. This causes them to turn too abruptly and forces them to slide low after the gate (see Figure 8.5).

CORRECTION

1. Remind racers that they want to be fast past each gate, not just to the gate.
2. Set line markers and outside poles for visual cues, and have racers look ahead.
3. Focus racers on turning at the line markers instead of right at the gates.

runs) or set two or three separate courses in a row down the hill. Each course should have a consistent but different rhythm than the previous course.

Coaching Point. Have your racers begin their turning phase at each line marker. As the skiers gain experience and an effective track is established, remove the line markers to see if your racers can continue on the proper line.

Variation. As your skiers gain proficiency, move to steeper terrain, repeating the same basic drill. The turns you set on the steep should be rounder, requiring more turn completion, than what you set on the flats.

Rhythm and Terrain Changes

Rarely are race courses set with consistent turns on consistent terrain from start to finish. Variations in terrain and rhythm challenge the racer to maintain speed by adjust-

ing the line. Your skiers will need to recognize and adapt to changes on the course.

Adapting to Rhythm Changes

Course setters vary the rhythm of courses by adjusting gate placement. The two most common rhythm changes are "fall line to round" turns, where a section of gates set down the fall line is followed by a section of gates set across the hill, and the opposite, "round to fall line" turns. In addition, slalom's unique gate combinations of flushes and hairpins are set specifically to test the ability of the racers to adjust to changes in rhythm.

Fall Line to Round Turns

Gates set across the fall line require the racer to aim higher than for gates in the fall line. The transition from straighter, more direct turns to rounder turns can be smooth if the racer is looking ahead and can anticipate the rhythm change (see Figure 8.6). Racers should

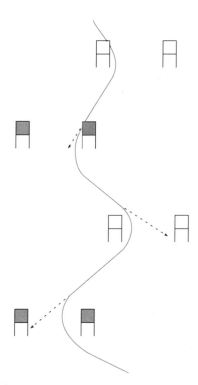

Figure 8.6   In "fall line to round" turns, a section of gates set down the fall line is followed by a section of gates set across the hill.

begin adjusting their line two gates before the first round turn. That way they can avoid harsh moves or skidding and maintain their momentum.

Round to Fall Line Turns

Changing from round turns to fall line turns requires letting the skis run a little bit straighter (still not directly at the gate) as the turns get straighter. The tempo may increase a little as well. Sometimes racers concentrate so hard on the more difficult turns that they forget to relax their line as the course straightens out (see Figure 8.7).

Slalom Combinations

Hairpins (two closed gates in a row) and flushes (three closed gates in a row) require their own special racing tactics. Slalom combinations significantly quicken the tempo, because they are set close together and straight down the fall line. The two components of slalom combinations you need to teach are the entry and exit.

The Entry.   Racers must line up their skis with the combination to enter it properly. If

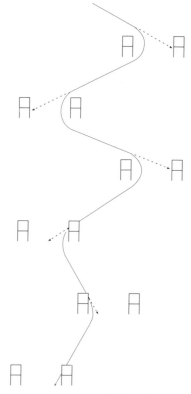

Figure 8.7   In "round to fall line" turns, a section of gates set across the hill is followed by a section set down the fall line.

their skis are aiming across the hill as they approach the first gate of the combination, the turn through it will be very sharp and difficult (see Figure 8.8). By lining up the skis

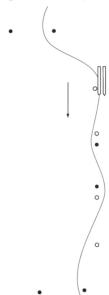

Figure 8.8   In slalom, skiers should line up their skis with the first gate as they approach a combination.

first and entering the combination balanced and slightly forward, the racer is ready for the quickness and only need make small turns.

The Exit. Because speed is generated by the quick turns in the combination, most course setters will try to slow the course down after a hairpin or flush by setting rounder turns. If a racer waits until after exiting the combination to begin to adjust the line, it may be too late. Instruct your skiers to round out the last turn of the combination so that their skis are pointed in the proper direction as they exit the hairpin or flush (see Figure 8.9).

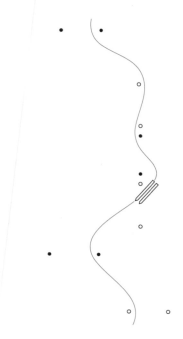

Figure 8.9 As skiers exit a combination, they should round out the last turn so that their skis are pointed in the proper direction for the next gate.

Drills for Rhythm Changes

Name. **Fall Line to Round Turns**

Purpose. To teach adapting to changes when the gates change from straight down the hill to across the hill.

Organization. Choose a smooth intermediate slope. Set a 10-gate course with the first 5 gates in the fall line and the next 5 out of the fall line. Each half should be consistent, so

the only rhythm change is the transition. Use line markers for the last two fall line turns and the first two round turns to establish a good track. Remove them to see if your skiers continue on the correct line.

Coaching Point. Racers must learn to recognize course changes for themselves. Line markers will not be there in races to point the way.

Name. **Round to Fall Line Turns**

Purpose. To practice the course change from round turns to straighter turns.

Organization. Choose a smooth intermediate slope. Set five round turns with line markers. Set a second 5-gate course in the fall line directly below the first one. Let your racers run each a few times. Then reset and make one course with five gates set across the fall line, followed by five straighter gates.

Coaching Point. Have your racers experiment to see where they can begin to straighten out their line and still ski the last five gates well.

Name. **Slalom Combinations**

Purpose. To adapt to the quickness of hairpins and flushes.

Organization. On a fairly flat, smooth section of an intermediate slope, set a 10-gate course, made up of 4 open gates, then a hairpin, followed by 4 more open gates (see Figure 8.10). Make all gates except the hairpin as rhythmical as possible. Reset, reversing all gates, to practice entering hairpins from each direction. Repeat with a flush instead of with a hairpin.

Coaching Point. Use a line marker 1 or 2 meters above the first pole of the combination to guide racers properly into it. Use another one at the first gate following the combination.

Adapting to Terrain Changes

The two main terrain changes you need to train your skiers to look for and adapt to are flats to steeps and steeps to flats. Both require adaptation of the line and may involve technical adjustments as well. Isolate and practice these situations so your racers will be able to recognize and adjust for them.

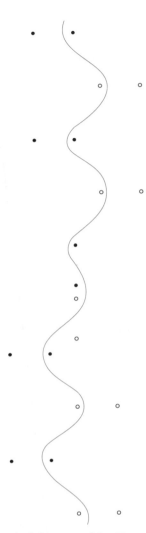

Figure 8.10 A slalom combination of open gates and a hairpin.

Steep is a relative term. The steep slope appropriate for young skiers should be challenging but well within their limits.

SKI TIP

When young ski racers practice gates, choose terrain they can handle easily. Slopes that are too steep reinforce braking, while flat slopes allow young racers to search for speed with confidence.

From Flats to Steeps

As a racer crests a knoll from a flat area to a steeper slope, two things happen. First, the pressure of the skis on the snow lessens significantly. When the pressure lessens, the skis momentarily get lighter. Since it takes pressure to turn skis, a racer trying to turn when the skis are light will slide instead of carve. Therefore, skiers must finish the turn and change direction completely by the time they crest a knoll. That way, even if the skis get light, they will already be aimed in the proper direction.

The other thing that happens when a skier crests a knoll is that the weight shifts back, which eliminates pressure on the front of the ski and leaves the skier with little control. To prevent this, your racers must make a conscious effort to be in good balance with arms forward as they approach a knoll. As they crest it, they need to press forward with their arms and hips. This will help them maintain pressure and snow contact. Instead of recovering, they will be in a great position to attack the hill.

To help the racers maintain speed and control, most course setters set courses a little straighter on the flats and rounder on the steeps. Rather than make line adjustments all at once (as they hit the steep section), skiers should adjust their line two gates before approaching the knoll. A higher line is needed because gravity will exert more of a force when the racer is skiing on the steeps. Steeps are much easier to ski when the racer starts out on the right line. It is very difficult to regain the line lost on the steeps.

From Steeps to Flats

As the hill flattens out, the course usually will straighten out, too. Racers approaching the flatter section can let their skis run a little more and usually can straighten out their line a bit as well. The racer who continues to make round turns on the flats will be slow. Racers who look ahead and adjust the line to the turn size and terrain give themselves the best chance for a fast time.

Drills for Adapting to Changing Terrain

Name. **Flats to Steeps**

Purpose. To learn to adjust the line when moving on to steeper pitches.

Organization. Find a steep pitch preceded by a flat section. Set six even-rhythm gates on the flat preceding a knoll, then continue setting over the knoll and down the pitch another six gates. Set line markers to show your racers where to begin to adjust the line two gates prior to the knoll. Reset often, after every three to four runs. Eliminate line markers if you think your racers understand. Replace the line markers, if your skiers need them.

Coaching Point. Inspect tracks with your skiers to help them see the effects of line; it is easy to distinguish the low lines from the correct line.

Name. **Steeps to Flats**

Purpose. To adjust the line approaching the flats.

Organization. Find a section of the hill that starts out steep and then flattens out. Set six gates at the bottom of the steep pitch, then continue on another six gates across the flats. Set a second course next to the first one, and have a small-scale dual competition to see who can carry the speed across the flats.

Coaching Point. The dual courses will encourage speed in a fun way.

Teaching Racing Tactics

With a progressive learning system, your skiers have the chance to practice skills in small doses and learn the tactics necessary for ski racing. Their ski racing skills and confidence will improve as you guide them through these progressions.

Organizing a Tactical Skills Progression

You can cover a tactical skills progression in a few weeks, as a buildup to a big race, over the course of a season, or over several years. If you coach entry-level skiers, you will probably want to stick with early stages of the progression. If your racers are more experienced, you may spend more time in advanced drills. However, even top racers repeat the beginning of the progression at the start of a new year and review many of the elements during the race season.

A tactical skills progression will incorporate the following steps:

- Short, simple courses
- Gradual introduction of rhythm and terrain changes
- Longer runs and more mileage
- Sprint training
- Race rehearsal

Giant Slalom Progression

Giant slalom provides a base for all the other events and is beneficial for the overall development of your ski racers, as both skiers and competitors. GS is the event to emphasize

---

Error Detection and Correction for Handling Terrain Changes

Sometimes when skiing a steep section, racers' lines get lower and lower at each gate until they are too low to make a gate and aren't able to complete their run.

ERROR	CORRECTION
The racer, forgetting about gravity, takes too direct a line onto and down the steeps.	1. Remind the racer to look ahead to get ready for the steep pitch.
	2. Instruct the racer to complete the direction change before cresting the knoll; the line must be higher than normal once on the steep.
	3. Place line markers on two or three gates leading to the knoll to assist the racer with finding the correct line.

the most with developing ski racers. This progression should be covered over the course of a season, with sections repeated as necessary.

Start with short, simple, even-rhythm courses:

√ Set some with round turns, others that are more in the fall line.
√ Set some on moderate terrain, others on flat terrain.
√ Use bamboo poles and do not allow skiers to hit the gates.
√ Use line markers until a track is established.
√ Have your racers look ahead when inspecting courses.

Add rhythm changes, on moderate consistent terrain:

√ Run round to fall line turn drills.
√ Run fall line to round turns drills.
√ Set an hourglass course: round turns to fall line turns, back to round turns.
√ Set the opposite: fall line turns to round turns, back to fall line turns.
√ Use line markers and inspect tracks with your racers.

Add terrain changes, keeping rhythm as even as possible:

√ Set 10-gate course on flats.
√ Set 10-gate course on steeps (as appropriate for your racers' level).
√ Then set 5 gates on flats continuing over a knoll with 5 gates on steep.
√ Then set opposite: begin on steeps and go to flats.
√ Expand to 15 or 20 gates with more than one terrain change.
√ Use line markers and inspect tracks with your racers.

Increase to half-length courses, with variety of terrain and rhythm changes:

√ Use line markers sporadically, as needed.

Begin incorporating sprint training occasionally with skills skiers have already mastered, that is, short simple courses:

√ Sprint courses—short, easy courses on the flats
√ Dual head-to-head courses—identical courses set at least 8 meters apart

Increase to full-length courses, with variety:

√ Racers should try to finish every course.
√ Time runs with a stopwatch to see how your racers are progressing.
√ Time two sections, one flat and one steep, to see how your racers are doing on each.

Make race rehearsal just like race day:

√ Long careful inspection of a full-length, flagged course
√ Two timed runs

Slalom Progression

Always precede slalom gate training with a review of slalom skiing skills as a warm-up. This puts your skiers into the rhythm of the quick turns they'll have in slalom courses. Slalom skiing skills to emphasize are the following:

- Linked, complete, quick turns at a consistent speed
- Arms up in front, upper bodies facing down the hill, weight forward
- Pole plants

Because of the quickness of slalom, line markers can be more confusing than helpful in slalom. The one place to use them is in the first few gates to help your racers find the line and rhythm right out of the start. This progression starts with cones and stubby gates before graduating to regular long poles. Racers can concentrate on making good turns and finding the correct line without the distraction of long poles. As they become comfortable, graduate to long poles. Like the GS progression, this progression can be covered over a season with sections repeated as necessary.

Start with cones:

√ Set 8 to 12 cones on even-rhythm courses.

Move to stubby gates:

√ Begin with 12- to 15-gate even-rhythm courses.
√ Introduce rhythm changes—first hairpins, later flushes.

Alternate stubbies with long flex poles:

√ Set a 12-gate course with long poles on right, stubbies on left.
√ Set a 12-gate course with stubbies on right, long poles on left.
√ Set a course with long poles for most gates, stubbies for rhythm changes.

For long flex poles, repeat the sequence as with giant slalom:

√ Start with short, simple courses.
√ Add rhythm changes (hairpins and flushes) gradually.
√ Add terrain changes.
√ Work up first to half-length; run these most frequently.
√ Train full-length courses; finish every course.
√ Use sprint work, especially short sprint courses.
√ Finish with a race rehearsal.

Speed Elements Training

Young racers may not yet be racing downhill and super-g, but they can benefit from training the elements of the speed events to gradually build skills. Teaching speed skills takes experience, because decisions have to be made about speed and safety. Include speed elements training in your program, but don't coach it by yourself at first. Make arrangements with an experienced coach to help you out—both you and your racers will benefit!

> ### SKI TIP
>
> Experienced slalom racers on a fast tight line avoid slamming their bodies into the gates by clearing slalom gates out of the way with their arms. Sometimes beginning skiers want to emulate more experienced racers whose lines put them close to the gates, but when inexperienced skiers reach to hit gates that aren't in their way, their tails skid out and slow them down. Racers should clear *only* gates that are directly in their path as a result of good turns. Emphasize to your racers that good turns come first.
>
> As your racers progress and their skis get closer to the gates, clearing gates becomes necessary. The best way to clear slalom poles is to keep the arms up in front and block without making any extra arm movements. Slalom poles give easily when hit (see Figure 8.11).
>
>
>
> **Figure 8.11** Clear slalom gates by keeping the arms up in front in a blocking position.

Speed elements can be trained at any ski area. A big mountain is not necessary to teach skiers some of the basic skills found in the speed events. The skills need not be practiced at high speed. At the introductory level, speed should be closely controlled and skills continually emphasized.

Your attitude as the coach can affect the safety of your racers in speed elements training. The environment you create must be fun and nonintimidating. Limit terrain so your skiers can search for speed, instead of braking to control it. Start easy, and add speed gradually to expand your racers' comfort zones. Quality, not quantity, should be emphasized. Remember, in every aspect, safety takes precedence.

Speed Elements Drills

Name. **Gliding Turns**

Purpose. To teach gliding skills.

Organization. Choose a flat, gentle slope. Start racers in a straight run, edge both skis in the same direction, weight the outside ski, and ride the edged ski until both skis are in a traverse. Then have them roll skis onto the new edges, shift weight to the new outside ski, and ride it in the new direction. Repeat, linking several of these turns together.

Coaching Point. There should be no pivoting or twisting, just the steering of the skis with the edges. These turns are more gradual than regular turns, but very smooth. Remind your skiers to keep the arms up and forward to maintain balance as speeds increase.

Variation. Repeat the same drill in a tuck. Keep the outside ski weighted and the turns clean.

SKI TIP

Safety takes precedence in all speed elements training. The slope used for speed elements training should be closed off from the public, and protection (reinforced fencing) used where necessary. The limiting factor for speed training will be the skill level of your skiers. They must have a strong technical base and the ability to listen well and to concentrate. Helmets are mandatory for all speed event training.

Name. **Super-g Turns**

Purpose. To introduce the larger, rounder turns of super-g.

Organization. Choose a wide intermediate slope. Set sections of 6-8 turns in an area where you might normally set 10 giant sla-

lom turns. For each turn, set two gates in a row to form a corridor (see Figure 8.12). Set the gates across the fall line to control speed.

Coaching Point. Exposure to a larger turn size and more gradual shape is more important than increased speed in this drill. By setting the corridors, your skiers can use the top gate of each pair of gates as a rise line and can more easily adapt to the new size turn.

Variation. Use corridors to work on gliding turns of the flats.

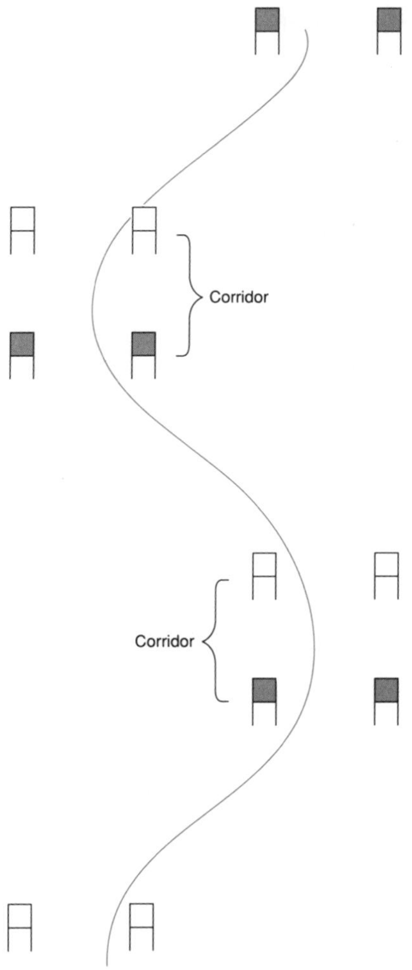

Figure 8.12 Use corridors to help racers feel the larger, rounder shape of super-g turns.

Visual Skills for Ski Racing

To adapt to course changes effectively, racers must be aware of what's ahead. Inspecting courses and looking ahead are two skills that allow your racers to ski their fastest from top to bottom.

Course Inspection

Before every race, competitors are given time to inspect the course carefully. Ski racers aren't allowed to practice on the course before racing it (except in downhill where it is mandatory), so course inspection is very important. During inspection, have your racers sideslip slowly through the course, looking at gate placement and course conditions, especially noting any rhythm or terrain changes. Have racers stop and study difficult sections extra carefully. This inspection will help racers get an overall feel for the course as well as a close look at challenging sections.

Inexperienced racers aren't always sure what to look for. Most coaches inspect race courses with their young racers, pointing out the challenging sections. As you become familiar with your ski racers' strengths and weaknesses, you'll get better at knowing what to point out. Remember, there is only so much a racer can think about on race day with so much excitement in the air. Resist the impulse to point out everything. Instead focus on a few basic things.

Looking Ahead

When skiing through a race course, a racer has to know where the course is going, where the gates are, and what the terrain is like ahead. Too many racers take the course moment by moment and look no farther ahead than the approaching gate. When they come upon a change in rhythm or terrain, it may be too late to make adjustments.

Racers must always be aware of what's ahead. In giant slalom, they can look ahead by briefly glancing two gates down the hill between turns. After glancing down the hill, the skier focuses on the upcoming gate. This way the racer knows what the next two gates look like and can prepare. In slalom, the turns are quicker, but the racer should have upcoming gates in his or her field of vision to be aware of upcoming situations.

Looking ahead is not natural for many racers. Have your skiers practice looking ahead every time they inspect a practice course. It's a skill that will improve quickly with practice.

Starts and Finishes

Before the first race, spend some time familiarizing your racers with start and finish procedures. This can be the most nerve-racking time for beginning racers, but your calm tone and direction will give them encouragement and support.

Starts

Races are timed electronically, and every race start is set up the same way. The racer stands on a flat platform behind a thin start wand attached to a post. In front of the wand, the hill slopes down to the race course. To start, the racer's feet are behind the wand with her poles planted in front and a few inches below (see Figure 8.13).

Figure 8.13 At the start, feet should be behind the start wand, the poles in front.

The start official gives the racer a 10-second warning, then either counts down (5-4-3-2-1-Go!) in giant slalom, or gives a "ready . . ." followed by a "hup" as soon as the skier starts in slalom. To start, the racer leans the upper body out over her poles, then pushes off. The heels lift up and the skis slide forward out of the start. The clock starts as the racer's shins touch the start wand, springing it open and triggering the timing (see Figure 8.14).

Finishes

The timing stops when the racer crosses the finish line. Emphasize to your racers to keep pushing until they are well past the finish

Figure 8.14 To start, a racer leans forward and pushes off, lifting the heels.

line. Normally, the fastest way to the finish from the last gate is to skate, but if racers are carrying a lot of speed, skating isn't necessary (see Figure 8.15).

To develop powerful starts and finishes, your racers should practice frequently. In every practice course include a start, by adding two poles about 1 meter apart at the top of the course, and a finish (two more poles about 10 meters apart).

Figure 8.15 A racer skates across the finish line.

Race Day

A coach's job on race day is to help skiers stay warm, loose, and focused. Most likely your racers will be excited and nervous. You can have a positive calming effect on them if you are well organized, upbeat, and relaxed. Set a race day routine that your athletes become familiar with; practice this in race rehearsals. Your race day routine should include organizational things like handing out numbers and explaining the time schedule and any rules specific to the particular event. The race day routine should also include a warm-up course, inspection of the race courses, and meeting with your skiers after each run.

Race day is not the time to teach technique and tactics. This method only overloads and confuses kids. The skills your racers have on race day are the ones they will use. If you have done a good job teaching tactics, your skiers should be able to recognize the various situations presented in the course. Your job during inspection is to point out difficult spots, remind your skiers how these situations should be handled, and keep them confident and focused.

After the race, give feedback to each skier, remembering to point out positives as well as ways to improve. Your skiers should have performance goals, not just outcome goals, for each race. Still, when they see their times, you may need to put performances into perspective for some of your racers. Be most attentive to those who have had a tough day; they need and deserve your support.

Even though ski racing is an individual sport, the camaraderie of teammates is important. Encourage your skiers to cheer and help each other out by carrying each others' extra clothes and supporting one another. A racer who is unhappy with a performance can bounce back quickly with supportive teammates. When a racer wins, the entire team can share in the victory. The friendships that develop will provide lasting memories for years to come. These friendships are a big part of what makes ski racing so much fun for kids and coaches!

Skiing and Coaching Books

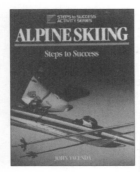

Alpine Skiing

Steps to Success

John Yacenda, PhD

1992 • Paper • 176 pp
Item PYAC0455
ISBN 0-88011-455-X
$13.95 ($17.50 Canadian)

Alpine Skiing: Steps to Success minimizes the time it takes to learn to ski. Step by step and at their own pace, students will acquire the knowledge and skills they need to ski safely, develop mental resolve, adapt to varying terrain, and act courteously on the slopes. They'll soon experience the satisfaction of becoming an accomplished alpine skier.

High Performance Skiing

John Yacenda, PhD

1987 • Paper • 312 pp
Item PYAC0288 • ISBN 0-88011-288-3
$16.95 ($20.95 Canadian)

This guide will help skiers gain the confidence and versatility to conquer any slope! It's packed with advice on skiing in steep terrain, all types of weather, and snow conditions. Author John Yacenda draws on the expertise of professional skier Mike Iman and other experts to provide readers with up-to-date tips for warming up, physical conditioning, and mental preparation for skiing the more advanced slopes.

Ski Games

A Fun-Filled Approach to Teaching Nordic and Alpine Skills

Laurie Gullion, MS

1990 • Paper • 192 pp
Item PGUL0367 • ISBN 0-88011-367-7
$16.95 ($20.95 Canadian)

With *Ski Games*, children can learn basic skills faster, develop more confidence, and enjoy skiing more in a carefree, noncompetitive environment. It will enable you to teach skiing playfully and positively, excite children about skiing and develop solid skiers at young ages, teach specific skills through activities that focus on those skills, identify common problems and make improvements, and teach different age groups.

Coaching Young Athletes

**Rainer Martens, PhD,
Robert W. Christina, PhD,
John S. Harvey, Jr., MD, and
Brian J. Sharkey, PhD**

1981 • Paper • 224 pp
Item BMAR0024 • ISBN 0-931250-24-2
$18.00 ($22.50 Canadian)

Coaching Young Athletes introduces and explains the basics of coaching, such as coaching philosophy, sport psychology, sport pedagogy, sport physiology, sports medicine, parent management, and sport law. You'll find exercises, examples, discussion topics, illustrations, and checklists designed to make learning how to be a more effective coach interesting and enjoyable.

ACEP Volunteer Level

The American Coaching Effectiveness Program (ACEP) now provides two excellent youth coaches' courses: the Rookie Coaches Course and the Coaching Young Athletes Course. The Rookie Coaches Course not only introduces coaches to the basic principles of coaching, but also teaches them how to apply those fundamentals as they instruct young athletes in the rules, skills, and strategies of their particular sport. The *Rookie Coaches Ski Racing Guide* serves as a text for the course.

The second coaching education option at the Volunteer Level is the Coaching Young Athletes Course. This alternative is for coaches who have completed the Rookie Coaches Course successfully and coaches who want to receive more instruction in the principles of coaching than is offered in that course.

ACEP encourages youth sport coaches to complete both the Rookie Coaches and Coaching Young Athletes Courses. We believe the combined learning experiences afforded by these courses will give you the coaching background you need to be the kind of coach kids learn from and enjoy playing for. Call the National Center at 1-800-747-5698 for more information on the ACEP Volunteer Level.

Prices are subject to change.

Place your credit card order today! (VISA, AMEX, MC)
TOLL FREE: U.S. (800) 747-4457 ■ Canada (800) 465-7301
OR: U.S. (217) 351-5076 ■ Canada (519) 944-7774
FAX: U.S. (217) 351-1549 ■ Canada (519) 944-7614

Human Kinetics Publishers
P.O. Box 5076 • Champaign, IL 61825-5076